EYE to THE SKY

Viewing the Great Pyramid of Khufu—Cheops—on the Giza Plateau near Cairo, Egypt, was a transformative experience for me. This is my personal photo of The Great Pyramid of Khufu and the lesser pyramid, July,1993.

EYE to THE SKY
STORYtELLING On tHE EDGE OF MAGIC

A memoir by three-time Emmy Award-winner

BOBBY NORFOLK

Parkhurst Brothers Publishers

MARION, MICHIGAN

www.parkhurstbrothers.com

Parkhurst Brothers books are distributed to the trade through the Chicago Distribution Center, and may be ordered through Ingram Book Company, Baker & Taylor, Follett Library Resources and other book industry wholesalers. To order from Chicago Distribution Center, phone 800-621-2736 or send a fax to 800-621-8476. Copies of this and other Parkhurst Brothers, Inc., Publishers titles are available to organizations and corporations for purchase in quantity by contacting Special Sales Department at our home office location, listed on our website. Manuscript submission guidelines for this publishing company are available at our website.

Printed in the United States of America First Edition, 2015

2016 2017 2018 2019 2020   16 15 14 13 12 11 10 9 8 7
6 5 4 3 2 1

Library of Congress Cataloging in Publication Data is pending

ISBN: Hardback, guaranteed library binding   978-1-62491-046-3
ISBN: Trade Paperback   978-1-62491-047-0
ISBN: e-book   978-1-62491-048-7

Parkhurst Brothers Publishers supports the First Amendment of the Constitution of the United States of America and believes that the free exchange of ideas is necessary for a people to remain free.

Cover and interior design by: Linda D. Parkhurst PhD
Photographs in this book are predominantly archival images from the author's personal files, for which no photo credit was available at the time of publication. The cover photographs of the author are the work of:
                              Neal Page Photography
Acquired for Parkhurst Brothers, Inc., Publishers
and edited by: Ted Parkhurst
Proofread by: Bill and Barbara Paddack

022016

DEDICATION

To my parents, Pauline and Willie Floyd Norfolk, with gratitude for their jokes and memories of their childhood in West Tennessee and Arkansas,

To my son Damon, his wife Monique, and their cutie-pie-clever daughter Mikaylah,

To my wife, Sherry, for her loving kindness, energy, creativity, brilliance, and inspiration,

To my brothers, Wilbert, and Paul O'Neil,

Special thanks to my extended family, the Buckleys, Harpers, Wrights, and Butlers,

To Jan Dolan, for helping to keep my career moving forward,

To Tim (TJ), Jenmougin, my computer wizard, the Steven Spielberg look-alike who keeps us online.

And Thank You

To Christa Ikard and Victoria Johnson for proofreading and typing

To gifted students at Jefferson Middle School, Springfield, IL for their inspiring words to write the book

CONTENTS

PREFACE
Growing Up 10

CHAPTER ONE
Early Years and Building the Imagination 15

CHAPTER TWO
Theatre of the Mind 18

CHAPTER THREE
My Early World 19

CHAPTER FOUR
Extended Family 22

CHAPTER FIVE
Superboy of Enright Avenue 26

CHAPTER SIX
Eugene Field Elementary School 31

CHAPTER SEVEN
The Batmobile and the Mack Truck 33

CHAPTER EIGHT
The Ice Age 38

CHAPTER NINE
Watch What You Think 41

CHAPTER TEN
Flash Flood in Cuivre River State Park 44

CHAPTER ELEVEN
Tear the Roof Off the Sucker 49

CHAPTER TWELVE
The Marvel Comics Group 51

CHAPTER THIRTEEN
April 4, 1968   54

CHAPTER FOURTEEN
Memories of Sumner High School   60

CHAPTER FIFTEEN
Ambushed at Dinner   63

CHAPTER SIXTEEN
Fish Eye, Politics, and Malcolm X   66

CHAPTER SEVENTEEN
Vietnam and the Beginning of Activism   73

CHAPTER EIGHTEEN
The Windy City   75

CHAPTER NINETEEN
Awakening the Sleeping Giant   78

CHAPTER TWENTY
Moving the Cat   87

CHAPTER TWENTY-ONE
Moonlighting as the Real Me   89

CHAPTER TWENTY-TWO
Up in Smoke   98

CHAPTER TWENTY-THREE
Call 911   114

CHAPTER TWENTY-FOUR
Python in the Night Club   117

CHAPTER TWENTY-FIVE
The Black Repertory Company of St. Louis   121

CHAPTER TWENTY-SIX
The Mountain Goat in Me   123

CHAPTER TWENTY-SEVEN
My Dinner With John John 136

CHAPTER TWENTY-EIGHT
Whoa—Big Boy! 141

CHAPTER TWENTY-NINE
This "New Thing Called Storytelling" 142

CHAPTER THIRTY
I Don't Know If I Hit Forty or Forty Hit Me 148

CHAPTER THIRTY-ONE
The Aurora Borealis at 35,000 Feet 150

CHAPTER THIRTY-TWO
Critter Encounters 154

CHAPTER THIRTY-THREE
The Vizsla and The Doggie Slobber 159

CHAPTER THIRTY-FOUR
Tension in the Foyer 161

CHAPTER THIRTY-FIVE
Discoveries on a Not-So-Dark Continent 164

CHAPTER THIRTY-SIX
First Comes Love 173

CHAPTER THIRTY-SEVEN
Swan Song 174

CHAPTER THIRTY-EIGHT
Alaskan Adventures in Storytelling 178

CHAPTER THIRTY-NINE
The Elephant and the Dandelion 184

CHAPTER FORTY
Attack of the Killer Holsteins 188

CHAPTER FORTY-ONE
Bell Rock 191

CHAPTER FORTY-TWO
Big Cats and Little Stars 193

CHAPTER FORTY-THREE
The Popcorn Box or Bobby in the Lobby 195

CHAPTER FORTY-FOUR
Niagara Falls 198

CHAPTER FORTY-FIVE
Mt. Bromo, East Java, Indonesia 199

CHAPTER FORTY-SIX
Ball Lightning 203

CHAPTER FORTY-SEVEN
Tinkerbelle 205

CHAPTER FORTY-EIGHT
Hagrid's Bug 206

CHAPTER FORTY-NINE
The Hood 210

CHAPTER FIFTY
The Visual Beauty on the Windward Shore of Oahu 212

CHAPTER FIFTY-ONE
Bats in the Belfry 216

CHAPTER FIFTY-TWO
Sharing the Fire 217

STORY AND THE SUBCONSCIOUS MIND
An Afterword 221

PREFACE
Growing Up

IN 1975, I WAS A SENIOR at the University of Missouri-St. Louis and facing a defining moment, a significant passage in my life. As a black militant and avid student of U.S. History, I was actively involved in consciousness-raising among black students and radical white students on the college and university campuses in the St. Louis area.

Then ... the movement died. African-American leaders had either been assassinated, exiled, imprisoned, seen their reputations ruined by the FBI, or had abandoned the movement to enter the mainstream business world. Malcolm X had been assassinated ten years earlier. Nelson Mandela was languishing in a South African jail. In 1963, Medgar Evers had been killed because he sought voting rights for blacks. In 1968, Martin Luther King Jr. had been shot at a Memphis, Tennessee, motel, a scene I was unable to erase from my active memory.

A young black radical, I was losing role models at an alarming rate. Where was I to look? Out of 537 members of the United States Congress, only *fourteen* were black. The governors of all fifty states were white. Colin Powell was still a student at the National War College that year. Outside of the U.S. Army, nobody had yet heard his name. Between 1932 and 1972, black men in Tuskegee, Alabama, had been secretly recruited to be treated like laboratory rats in a U.S. government test to determine the effects of the dreaded disease syphilis. In the test, penicillin, the known cure, was withheld from them so scientists could observe the advanced stages of the disease. A TV sitcom, *The Jeffersons* premiered in the 1970s featuring a black man whose buffoonery bordered on *Amos & Andy*. It would run for the next eleven years, and then go into syndication. Then *Good Times*, a sitcom—a caricature—of black life in the Chicago projects premiered. It's somewhat relevant setting and situations were over-powered by the over-the-top comedy of J.J. Kid, *Dynomite*!!!

The only bright spot—only role model who stood out for black youth that year—was a black kid from Richmond, Virginia, named Arthur Ashe. Ashe surprised a whole lot of folks by winning a tennis tournament at Wimbledon in England. I later found out Ashe attended his senior year at Charles Sumner High School in St. Louis, Missouri, the school I would attend several years later. I did not aspire to make my way in the world banging little yellow balls around a green rectangle.

I was not a rebel without a cause, but it sure looked like I was a rebel without a future.

What followed was a fallow period for me. Where could I succeed? What direction might lead to success? Was even a modest happiness to elude me and my generation? A restlessness stirred within; something that had long been pushed down wanted to rise to the surface. What could a lost, lonely, discouraged kid from the low-rent blocks of St. Louis do with the rest of his life?

I took on the study of world religions, especially Catholicism, Buddhism, Islam, and Judaism. I studied Krishna, Jesus, Moses, and spiritual mysticism. Going beyond religion, I also studied meta-physics, transcendental meditation, Hatha yoga, the martial arts, and vegetarianism. Given the dominant culture of mid-America, Jesus was an odds-on favorite for my attention. Jesus had hair like lamb's wool, like me, and could turn water into wine to keep the party going! He was kind of radical, too. He had a sharp comeback for every slur the Pharisees threw at him, yet when facing Herod, Jesus showed that he was a gentle soul. That appealed to me. Jesus could work a big room. In fact, his best work was done in front of so many people, he had to do it on the side of a mountain. *That* was pretty cool.

Moses did some amazing stuff on a big stage, too, and I admired his style. If I could just get my hands on a walking stick and turn it into a serpent—at will—that would wow any crowd. Plus, Moses had a moral authority that I envied. When he talked, people listened.

Buddha was a curious model. His followers' teachings about states of consciousness appealed to a generation that wasn't real pleased with the conscious world it found itself inhabiting. Buddhist teachings of tranquility and mindfulness especially appealed to me, because I sensed that tranquility would be at a premium in the social turmoil around me. I wanted to develop an inner strength, not to impress others, but as a foundation for a life as (to use a phrase coined a generation or two later) a *change agent.*

Each spiritual tradition was appealing, in its own way. Obviously, I could not be a Christian, a Jew, a Muslim, and a Buddhist at the same time. But by studying each of these traditions, I became *aware.* I found that awareness would serve me well, whoever I became. As a spiritual person who sought unceasing awareness, I opened myself to learn from everyone around me. A brother, mother, janitor, off-duty police officer, barber, out-of-work artist—all of these and many more became my teachers. Awareness opened my eyes, and I finally realized that we as humans are so busy trying to make a living, we've forgotten how to live.

The rock group, Earth, Wind & Fire, had come on the scene in 1973. By 1975, I was beginning to find messages in their music. They seemed to be saying that an entire way of thinking existed, one that I had not begun to explore. Their 1975 tune, "Reasons," spoke to the emptiness I felt. When Phillip Bailey sang, "I can't find the reasons," he was addressing me, not about love lost, but knowledge and wisdom gained.

I was beginning to form a personal foundation for the way ahead. I decided to begin on a path to self–realization, even if it meant carving out a way that made sense only to me. I would determine my *purpose for being*. Some mystics say that through spiritual searching we awaken a sleeping giant within us. They say that once it is awakened, The Master Within cannot go back to sleep. To follow him, they seemed to say, we unleash an insatiable hunger for wisdom, knowledge, and illumination. Spiritually, I knew I was one hungry young man.

In 1975, I studied the Ancient Teachings of The Rosicrucian Order and learned about so-called hidden truths that rivaled the teachings of quantum physics and mechanics.

A writer and thinker I kept seeing on television shows, hearing on NPR, and having friends tell me about began to interest me. His books were about awareness, centering the soul, and deep knowledge. His name was Deepak Chopra. I was immediately engaged by his books and audio recordings, especially *The Way of the Wizard*. I was drawn to his writings about Merlin's teachings to the boy, Arthur, with whom I identified. During Arthur's apprenticeship to the wizard, Merlin, the old man taught that we humans start off as innocents. Merlin taught that we then develop in our spirit a thing called the ego. The ego can become big trouble. From there, he taught, we can continue in our development through several stages: first The

Achiever, then The Giver, The Seeker, and The Seer, until finally it is possible to become Pure Spirit. What follows in this book is my interpretation of that voyage of discovery as I have experienced it.

You will undoubtedly experience that voyage differently, but I hope that my experience will help open your eyes to possibilities and energies that may comfort you on your path.

CHAPTER ONE

Early Years and Building the Imagination

I WAS A SOLITARY CHILD. My toys were scraps of wood gathered from the alley. Empty cereal boxes were another favorite. I would take scissors and cut the cartoon characters from them to use as action figures in my play. Cereal boxes also became flat-top mesas from which toy cowboys could keep their eyes peeled for toy Indians who traipsed unsuspectingly below. I quickly devised a mountain peak from a triangular wood scrap. It added perspective to my elaborate battles between the toy cowboys and toy Indians that my parents bought at the nearby Woolworth's five and ten cent store. In the decade following World War II, when I was a preschooler, molded plastic soldiers shouldering M-1 rifles or bazooka anti-tank guns came in a variety of colors, two dozen to the dollar bag. Being a Pisces, I was capable of sitting on the living room floor and creating my own little world for two or three hours at a time. Human companionship was irrelevant; my nature fairies were right there with me.

A city kid, I was content to read comic books like *Casper the Friendly Ghost, Spooky The Tuff Ghost, Archie,* Bazooka Bubble Gum comics, and the funny papers from the *St. Louis Post-Dispatch* and *St. Louis Globe-Democrat.* Before attending public school, I had been introduced to books by the television shows *Captain Kangaroo* and *Romper Room.* I imagined adventures for my Lionel electric train set, its gleaming engine pulling a long chain of boxcars to remote parts

15

of Missouri, despite the steep grades of the mountains I knew lay somewhere to the west. I knew that somewhere beyond North St. Louis there grew beans whose stalks had been climbed by a fellow named Jack, even into the clouds. I had heard of a Corn Castle in a faraway land where a beautiful girl was stranded all alone in a tower, the location of which was kept secret by a mean old woman with a broken nose.

I spent hours sitting on the floor of my family's apartment, lost among the characters of books or making up crises for those characters in imaginative play. During those periods of wonder, I was actually hard at work as Captain of the Forces of Good, who struggled in a world repeatedly threatened by the Forces of Evil. As I later discovered, the work of children is play.

In spite of my parents' limited means, the apartment was not lacking in treasure troves. One treasure trove was my father's toolbox. Like all treasure chests, it had a lid that folded back once the nail was removed from the hasp on the front side. Once opened, it yielded not one but two layers of amazing implements suitable for imaginative play. As I lifted the first layer out by its handle, I was careful to keep it level. I couldn't have the glass-handled screwdrivers falling out on the floor! Underneath, I discovered a small saw, something called a "brace and bit" that rotated like a crank, and several tools whose names were unknown to me. Acting on impulse once when I was about seven, I borrowed my dad's ice pick from this tool box and carved an image of a cowboy on a horse into the cabinet of our Magnavox TV. When my mom saw it, she exclaimed, "Bobby, what is that?!"

Exasperated at having to state the obvious, I replied, "Art!"

A spanking and a fresh supply of butcher paper and crayons followed. Our butcher paper came out of an aluminum foil box that had been demoted to holding non-shiny wrap. But butcher paper was far superior to aluminum foil for drawing. Turning my attention to the thin box of eight crayons supplied with the butcher paper, I escaped into a reverie of awe. Admiring the perfectly pointed crayon ends, I imagined the potential to make green apples in the hands of a freckle-faced Archie, or broadswords in the hands of medieval knights. I eyeballed the first length of butcher paper my mother separated from the box as she stretched it diagonally across a thousand tiny teeth on the box edge.

I loved to take walks on the grass of the vacant lots behind our house. The bushes, with their attendant bees, beetles, and butterflies challenged me to catch a flying or hopping critter. In short order, I discovered that most flying insects were more than a match for my quick arms and hands. Despite that realization, the chase occupied me happily for hours on end. In those days, parents encouraged kids to *go out and play!*

There was no concern about abductions and kidnappings. Out-of-doors was a luxury for parent and child. The only rule on weekday evenings or weekends was to be home by dinnertime.

Exhausted from chasing butterflies, I could lie down on my back and gaze up through the branches of an oak tree for extended periods of time. As the grass tickled my back, my eyes darted from the tree limbs above to nearby flowerbeds. There, liver-colored critters shaped like drinking straws moved like living accordions, peeked out of the soil, and inched along through the mulch. Before I knew anything about fishing, earthworms entertained me among the flowers and bedding plants.

Returning my gaze to the world of tangled tree limbs above, I observed feathered parents tending their fuzzy young. I witnessed noisy disputes between squirrels over an acorn within reach, while I noticed a dozen similar acorns just a few branches away. The menagerie of squabbling squirrels, colorful birds, and winged bugs in those branches fed my curiosity. Watching them was all I needed to regenerate. Though I would not have known it at the time, immersing myself in that world also fed my spirit. Many years later, amid the stresses of career and relationships of adult life, I found myself returning to those childhood hours. At those times, I realized that my stage work benefited more than anything else by reliving that early awareness of the natural world. Communing with nature, whether observing competing eagles or staring at the stars, fed my soul and enlivened my storytelling.

CHAPTER TWO

Theatre of the Mind

MY EARLIEST EXPERIENCE of mass media was listening to the radio. We didn't get a television in our house until I was six. My family had settled on Kensington Avenue in North St. Louis, Missouri, in the mid-1940s. In 1951, when I was born, my daddy and mama moved with my older brother Wil and me all of two blocks away to 4545 Enright Avenue. The neighborhood had been romanticized in the movie *Meet Me in St. Louis* with Judy Garland, which was based on the 1904 World's Fair. We would see that movie many times in my childhood; it returned to local theatres again and again—whenever the new movies of the season had run their course.

What a fantastic opportunity for me to use my imagination as a *theatre of the mind* even though at that time I had no idea what I was experiencing was *reality*. We had a Magnavox radio as big as a chest of drawers. Our apartment was in a tenement house with four units. We were on the second floor, facing south. It was a small four-room space where Mom, Dad, older brother Wil, newborn Paul, and I lived.

CHAPTER THREE

My Early World

DAD RAN THE ELEVATORS at the department store Stix, Baer & Fuller. Mom worked in a Jewish confectionery owned by Dave Bean. Mr. Bean gave Mom a sack of groceries every day, a daily feast that she brought home for us boys and Dad. Mr. Bean would allow us to walk freely through the food shop and get candy, ice cream, soda pop, potato chips, and fruit.

If we wanted sandwiches, he would reach into the cold meats case, remove a log-shaped piece of bologna, salami, cheese, or whatever we wanted, turn on the slicer and cut off a few slices. The next thing we knew, he would be stacking everything between slices of bread and layering it up with mustard, lettuce, and tomato! What we could not eat in the store, he wrapped in butcher paper for us to take home.

Mom was a clerk at the food shop and waited on the customers. Mr. Bean tended the bar in the next room. Folks would come into the shop to buy groceries—or step into the bar for a tall, cold glass of beer there, before heading home for dinner. Kenneth Bean, Mr. Bean's son, always came into the shop after he got off work. I wasn't sure of his day job, but I did notice that he carried a pistol in a shoulder holster, half-hidden inside his suit coat.

Buddy Bean was the grandson who we envied as heir to the salami-and-beer fortune. We could not know then that just a few years later Buddy would set out on an adventure with his teenaged friends in a canoe on the Meramec River in St. Louis County, and never return. On that sad day—then still in the future—Buddy would tumble over the gunwale of the canoe, and be lost forever in the turbulence of the river below. Drowned in one of the infamous sinkholes where the river swirled back upon itself, Buddy lost his luck and his life. For weeks afterward, Mr. Bean's usual cheer was absent, and he went about his work in uncharacteristic silence.

My brothers and I often hopped the trolley car at The Ville and rode as it lumbered bumpily out Easton Avenue, now Martin Luther King Drive, to the village of Wellston. It was a three-mile adventure to the Bean confectionary. The trolley fare was five or ten cents, depending on your age.

From the trolley stop in Wellston Loop by KATZ Drugstore, we skipped the six blocks through the neighborhood of Craftsman-style bungalows to Mr. Bean's candy, salami, bologna, and beer emporium. Little brother Paul would dance on the bar for nickel tips, doing his imitation of vaudeville tap dancers while patrons chanted encouragement. It wasn't long before Paul perfected a tip-worthy routine, sure to elicit audience response, and end with a bulging pocketful of coins. Jabbing the air with elbows as he swayed first to the left, then to the right, along the bar, Paul bounced his knees with a lively rat-a-tat-tat. The sound effects were supplied by his shiny black shoes onto which a cobbler had nailed kidney-shaped metal "taps."

With no skills to demonstrate, Wil and I were envious of Paul's leaden pocketful of coins after his act.

The elevator that Dad operated at Stix, Baer & Fuller

Department Store (now Dillard's) seemed like a room to me then, large enough to contain four overstuffed easy chairs. Of course, it had no chairs, just a fold-down piano-stool kind of round seat on which dad could sit if he became weary navigating the four floors of the department store on Washington Boulevard. The elevator's double doors opened slowly as it settled at each floor. Its shining brass outer doors opened lazily to reveal an accordion-style screen inner door that Dad opened by hand, leaning across from his position at the button-studded control board on the side wall.

Always jovial and gregarious with a joke or witty line for customers, Dad beamed a big-toothed smile, announcing the floor number and its departments. If he disliked the routine nature of his work, Dad never expressed any disappointment to his boys. However, he did encourage us to perform at our best in studies and our extra-curricular activities.

At home in his easy chair, Dad loved Cardinal baseball on KMOX radio! Even though I did not particularly like professional baseball, I vividly remember Dad listening to the legendary Harry Caray and Jack Buck do their commentaries. When a member of the Cardinals would solidly connect with a ball, Harry Caray would say, "There it goes—waaaaay back. ... It could be—IT IS—a home run!" Dad loved *The Sporting News* baseball paper and read it religiously. It was his constant companion—that newspaper and a bottle of Budweiser. The paper would rustle as he opened it grandly, settling into a Sunday afternoon game, his cold drink standing at the ready on a side table at his elbow. Dad knew all the statistics of the players in both leagues. After a game, Dad would migrate to the front porch where I heard him discussing stats with friends, fathers of my friends who lived on our block.

CHAPTER FOUR

Extended Family

ALL FOUR OF MY GRANDPARENTS passed away before I knew them. As a child, Dad was taken in by Uncle Spencer Lewis Norfolk, twenty years older than Dad and principal of a primary school in Covington, Tennessee. Papa George, Spencer's father, was the family elder. Papa George was an ex-slave who then owned the farm where my daddy and Spencer grew up. The farm seemed enormous to me, with its house, outbuildings, barn and barnyard nestled in rolling hills that seemed infinite to a little boy. It was there that I saw pigs in the shade under the porch, chickens pecking in the dirt between the house and smokehouse. I played on the tire swing under a giant oak with cousins and ate homemade peach ice cream. Johnnie Mae Byers, Spencer's sister, moved to St. Louis along with everyone but Papa George and his wife, Charlotte.

Johnnie Mae was called "Big Mama" by all the children. Her only child was Georgia Bell Byers, fifteen years older than me. One day at Big Mama's house, the three of us boys refused to come in the house when Big Mama called several times. She told Georgia Bell to "go get those boys and bring them into the house."

Tired of having to come outside and round us up all the time, Georgia Bell decided to scare us inside. For her scary costume, she went into the closet and got one of Big Mama's old black dresses and a black Sunday hat with a veil. Right at the "dark thirty" (just before evening turns to night), she came around the alley moaning and wailing, "WOOO! Come here, little boys. WOOO WOO! I'm going to eat you. Woo. Woo!"

We screamed and ran—banging on the back door, shouting, "Big Mama Big Mama, let us in!" When Big Mama opened the door, we clung to her like paper clips to a magnet, clutching her legs and crying.

"What's wrong with you boys?"

All we could do was blubber. Shortly afterward, Georgia Bell came from the front room giggling and smirking. Big Mama knew Georgia Bell had tricked us. "You ought to be ashamed of yourself, scaring these boys like that."

Georgia Bell said, "I was tired of these hard-headed boys not minding ... and wanted to teach them a lesson."

After dinner, Mom and Dad regaled us with stories of their childhood, Dad growing up in Covington, Tennessee, and Mom in Crawfordsville, Arkansas, across the Big Muddy. Mom and Dad's stories and jokes remembered from childhood were funny and sometimes spicy. Dad would ask we boys at the dinner table, "Adam and Eve and Pinch Me Tight went over the river to see a fight. Adam and Eve came back before the fight. Who was left to see the fight?"

I would shout out, "Pinch Me Tight!" Responding as rapidly as a boxer's right punch, Dad reached out with a friendly but firm pinch on my arm.

Mom would say, "That's nothing; listen to this! A woman named Annie sent her clothes to a neighborhood laundry service. Her panties were always dirty when she picked them up. She wrote a letter to the owner: 'Dear Viney, please put more soap on panty. Signed, Annie.' The laundry owner replied by letter saying, 'Dear Annie, please put more soap on your hiney. Signed, Viney!'"

Dad would retort: "Why did the baby bottle of ink cry?" Because his Daddy was in the PEN, and he didn't know how long the sentence would be!"

Without losing a beat, Mom continued, "I knew a girl so skinny, she could hula hoop with a Cheerio!"

Dad, ever ready to get the last zinger in, replied, "I had a friend whose mother thought her son could do no wrong. One day when he was in the school marching band, she observed coyly, 'Oooooh look at my baby! Everybody is out of step but him!'"

At home, in that little dining room, there was an abundance of love and warmth, along with the smell of roasted pork, mustard greens, corn bread, and bubbly candied yams. Laughter was as sweet as the vanilla wafers and Neapolitan ice cream, our traditional dessert.

One night, I remember Mom concluding the mealtime story-telling with a story about a time she misbehaved. "When I was about ten years old," she said, "My daddy, whose name was Battle Locke, stood in front of his mule, while working on something on the other side of the barn. I got bored and started pulling on the mule's tail, jumping back giggling. Irritated, that mule kicked a back hoof out in anger, aiming right for me. Turning around in the barn just then, Daddy saw the mule kick and me fall backward in the dirt. The kick did not make contact, but daddy thought it had. Daddy scooped me up and ran into the house yelling, 'Mary, see about this girl.' Upset and angry, Daddy got his shotgun and started loading it with red, twelve-gauge shells. He was getting ready to go shoot the mule."

"Crying, I told Mama what really happened. She ran outside to catch daddy, who by now was aiming at that poor mule's head. 'Battle Locke! Leave that animal alone. That silly girl didn't get kicked. Besides, she told me she was pulling and yanking on his tail!'" The whole family hooted at that, pushing our chairs back from the table.

When the table was cleared, it was time for our radio shows. I gazed in wonder at the huge glass tubes inside the washing machine-sized wooden radio cabinet. My eyes locked onto the first warm light behind the radio dial, where wires inside pepper-shaker sized glass tubes began to glow very gradually. Several minutes of heating up was required before a signal kicked in. Once the tubes brightened to a golden glow, voices issued forth from the speakers. Programs such as the murder mysteries *The Inner Sanctum, The Shadow, The Lone Ranger,* the black comedy series *Amos and Andy,* the gangster shoot 'em up, *Gangbusters,* and the mind-bending, *The Creaking Door* were standards on the radio. I would sit in my Daddy's lap, and the power of radio would take me on a journey through the theatre of my mind.

My favorite was *The Shadow.* When it came on, a baritone voice would intone; "What evil lurks in the hearts of man? Only The Shadow knows. Moooo ahh ha ha ha haaaa!!!" It got my attention! The realism of the people talking and the action produced by the use of vivid sound effects was riveting. My family would turn the lights off in the apartment except for one to create a theatre-like atmosphere. I felt the action was taking place right there in the room. I forgot I was at home, but imagined I was wherever the characters were.

These craftsmen would create all the genres of entertainment: comedy, suspense, horror, gangster activity, westerns, and big band music. The series were episodic, meaning we would have to tune in the next night to find out what happened to the characters. This only heightened the senses, and I couldn't wait to find out what would happen next. This "reality" carried over to the time when Dad brought a television into the house. Then, "reality" took on an entirely different meaning.

CHAPTER FIVE

Superboy of Enright Avenue

FASTER THAN A SPEEDING BULLET … POW! More powerful than a loco-motive … chi-chi-chi-chiiii. Able to leap tall buildings in a single bound! Look up in the sky! It's a bird, it's a plane, it's Superman! Superman! Strange visitor from another planet, with powers and abilities far beyond those of mortal man. SUPERMAN—Who can change the course of mighty rivers; bend steel with his bare hands. And who, disguised as Clark Kent, a mild-mannered reporter working for a large metropolitan newspaper, fights the never-ending battle for Truth, Justice and the American Way!

I have a vivid memory of these incidents because Superman was my first introduction to the superheroes on television, in the papers, or radio. Watching those early episodes of Superman certainly challenged my child's sense of "reality" and confused my conception of "real" vs. imaginary.

When I was two and a half years old, I conducted a most interesting experiment with the force of gravity. The original Superman on TV starred George Reeves, and this show would burst onto the screen with a meteor exploding in a farm field, followed by a scene played out in imagined worlds above. I loved this series, as did my older brother. I would always take one of mom's hand towels and have my older brother, Wil, pin it on each shoulder of my white T-shirt. Along with my tighty-whities and white socks, the result was—Superman!

We would climb on top of our wooden chest of drawers and

do swan dives onto our beds. For the brief two seconds that I was airborne, I was indeed Superman! At least in my imagination.

Now, the reality check. My mom needed to take Wil to register him for kindergarten. Mom decided that the prudent thing was to leave me in the care of the babysitter, an elderly woman who lived down the hall in an apartment that smelled of cats. Dour statues of stern saints looked down from every shelf, every appliance, every chest of drawers and wall nook in the babysitter's apartment. Mom decided that anyone who lived with so many saints must surely exude the moral authority to keep one preschooler in check for sixty minutes.

The plaster-cast saints looked like The Joker in a card deck to me, unconvincing smiles painted badly into place. There was no way I was going to stay in that apartment while those two went off to an enchanted place called "kinder-garden school!" I had no idea why I couldn't go too. Summoning impeccable preschooler logic, I made my displeasure at this decision known. I wailed and threw a royal tantrum in protest, but to no avail. I definitely wasn't going with them. The babysitter was ancient, probably forty-five years old! My Mom was twenty-nine at the time, and her hair color was natural. Black folks in that era always paid respect and honor to any elder, so I felt trapped. Miss McNeil wore her customary uniform, a gaudy flowered dress, brown stockings that folded into a knot at the knees, big-framed glasses, and a bun hairdo. She took me down the hall to her place of statues. I was inconsolable after that, especially when Mom and Wil left.

Insensitive to my plight, Wil had a look of glee on his face. He was all dressed up in new clothes. Even at three and a half, I was seething with outrage and indignation! I could easily go back and forth from Miss McNeil's apartment to ours, so I rushed to my room and looked out the window, where I saw Mom and Wil disappearing down the street.

She had him by the hand and there they were, just casually strolling down Enright to Taylor Avenue and around the corner. The school, Eugene Field Elementary, was a fifteen-minute walk from the house. Field School was named after the famously moralistic children's poet and essayist.

My window overlooked the roof of the front porch. If you opened the window, you could step out onto the flat part of the roof from the second floor, facing the intersection they had just turned on. *That was when* the idea came to me, to use my Superman skills to fly to their destination and surprise them! I envisioned flying over their heads taunting them both, "Ha, ha! You can't keep me at home with a babysitter! I'm going to kinder-garden too!" So I tip-toed into my room and got my favorite white bath towel and two safety pins, and secured my cape. After checking on Miss McNeil to confirm that she was engaged in delicate needlework, I ran back to our apartment and into my room. As I climbed out onto the roof of the porch, I focused and tried to remember how Superman did it. I remembered.

He would run and jump with both of his hands out-stretched—and fly!

So, I measured my steps, and then took a running jump.

Time stood still. I didn't!

I felt myself falling in slow motion. I landed in a flower bed of loose, newly-dug dirt. The landlord had been preparing the flower bed in the front yard just below my window for the autumn. After I had plummeted downward, I gave an "umph" upon impact with the soft earth. My moaning continued. I felt fresh dirt in my face and mouth. In fact, my white outfit was now full of dirt and mud. Rolling onto my back, moaning in pain, I gasped for breath lost in my impact with the ground.

As God and fate would have it, I looked up to see a man sitting on his front porch across the street, staring at me in complete shock! He obviously had witnessed my less-than-super powered escapade.

Before I knew it, he had run across the street and was standing over me. Gently, he lifted me out of the mulch and carried me to my front door. Extending a fingertip, he rang the bell, summoning Miss McNeil. When Miss McNeil came downstairs and opened the front door, he asked her, "Who does this boy belong to?"

Miss McNeil's eyes were as large as hard-boiled eggs. She said, "How did he get outside?"

At his reply, "I saw him fall out of the window," she screamed in terror, realizing that the little Superman had been too fast for her. Examining me for broken bones and trauma, the two adults only found a small bloody cut on my right eyebrow. Miss McNeil took me from the man's arms, stammering, "Thank you, thank you, sir. I don't know how this happened!"

Before Mom got back home, Miss McNeil had dressed my wound with a cooling white ointment, washed me up, removed my dirty clothes, and dressed me in fresh underclothes. When Mom arrived, Miss McNeil sat beside my bed, watching and praying that I wouldn't die. She babbled to Mom about how sorry she was, explaining how I climbed out onto the roof of the front porch and tried to follow them. Mom washed my face all over again in the face bowl, dressed me in clean clothes, and took me by taxicab to Homer G. Phillips Hospital. That cut on my right eyebrow required six stitches. The doctor leaned over me so closely, I could see that he needed a shave. Then he told me in his kind, gentle manner that he was going to give me a shot with this little needle and my eyebrow would go numb. He said he did not want me to feel the stitches when he sewed my head up.

After ten minutes, the Novocaine kicked in, and the stubble-faced doctor proceeded to sew my eyebrow up. I felt the needle going in and out of my forehead, followed by the thread, but—strangely—I felt no pain. It was like I was witnessing a rag doll being sewn and looking on as a detached observer. The hospital smells I took in that day have never lost their familiarity. When I walk into a hospital today, the same chemicals aromas fill my nostrils, and I conjure up that childhood visit all over again in my mind. It was then I was made aware of how the five senses unlocked memory from the unconscious mind. The doctor recommended that Mom allow him to admit me there for overnight observation. When she considered leaving me again in a strange environment, her face colored, and she insisted on taking me home. The doctor disagreed vigorously. Mom looked at me with the bandage on my head. Then, she looked out the eleventh-floor window to the concrete parking lot below. She stood her ground. Not daring to leave me alone again, she told the doctor that she would assume all responsibility for my welfare, as the doctor would not. Mom checked me out with the doctor still shaking his head in disagreement. From the front steps of the hospital, we took a taxicab back home.

I had to be thinking by now; "This has to be much better than some stoopid kinder-garden!" At home, I got out my toy soldiers and started playing on the floor under Mom's constant gaze. Dad heard about my exploit when he got home. Holding me gently, Dad rocked me on his lap. His frequent sighs told me that he was relieved I hadn't broken my neck or back. At the table with my parents and brother, I ate dinner under their careful watch, as if they feared I might suddenly jerk my fork full of sweet peas and reopen my forehead wound. Then it was off to bed for the longest sleep of my young life. There were no recurring problems, except for the scar on my right eyebrow.

I knew Mom had regrets about leaving me with the sitter. Even then, I could tell she watched me more closely than ever. I didn't think she was concerned that I might jump out another window (well maybe she did believe that), but she wanted to be sure that the medical complications that the doctor feared did not develop. I never ever had another inclination to leap from a building in a single bound; I learned that lesson well. Years later, Mom recounted all of the details of this story. The more she said, the more amazed I was to have survived the fall.

CHAPTER SIX

Eugene Field Elementary School

WHEN I STARTED SCHOOL at Eugene Field Elementary, I was a stutterer. From kindergarten through tenth grade, I spoke with difficulty. Always in fear of being called on in class, I was equally worried on the playground. I feared having to speak, and spent most of the time in my own world. When kids made fun of me, I would retreat into books. I thought that if I had a book in my face the teachers wouldn't ask me to talk. Wrong! Because of a few caring and talented master teachers who refused to give up on me, my speaking difficulty was not politely overlooked. I was granted the chance to rise above my handicap because of several remarkable teachers, most of whom were alumni of segregated Harris-Stowe Teachers College in St. Louis. They saw things in me that I didn't see in myself. I'm not talking memorization or mathematical analytics or even language arts. The teachers Harris-Stowe turned out were gifted in finding diamonds—or at least pearls—buried deep inside ordinary, spindly, reticent children. Harris-Stowe graduates predominated on the faculty at Eugene Field Elementary, where I was enrolled. Their presence meant that my grade school was a place a pupil could be reasonably sure of finding an advocate—a teacher who cared enough to find out what competency may be hidden inside him.

The Harris-Stowe teachers I was lucky enough to have at Eugene Field Elementary made a consistent effort to discern in me the aptitudes that I didn't see in myself. Later, I learned that one mark of a master teacher is the ability—maybe it is intuition—to discern the latent potential of the child with low self-esteem, which was my one dominant trait at the time. My long suffering Harris-Stowe-trained teachers found creativity bottled up inside the scrawny kid I was at the time. And they set about polishing that bit of promise with tireless determination. One of the first things that gave me away, I'm convinced, was my habit of reading for enjoyment. When they figured out that I loved to read mysteries, detective stories, and biographies, they were adamant to unearth more promising traits that lay within my silent shell. I was fascinated by the quote on the back of our school book, *Reading for Comprehension,* written by St. Louis Schools Superintendent William Kottmeyer, .

Teachers, noticing how I was a voracious little reader, sensed a latent creativity worthy of cultivation. I guess I gave myself away volunteering for fourth-grade poetry recitals. It seemed like an innocent enough gesture, raising my hand to get a part in every opportunity to recite. But it proved to be a turning point not only in what the teachers knew about me, but also a major intersection in what I knew about myself. *I liked being on stage! The audience was there for me!*

In 1961, I kept hearing a new song playing on the radio.

The song was so enchanting that I memorized it. This spoken word ballad by Jimmy Dean was called "Big Bad John," the story of an uncommon "common" man. When I recited it from beginning to end, my teachers told me that I had not stuttered a bit—even on the chorus! It was a life-changing moment. From that day on, whenever I performed, I didn't stutter.

My teachers encouraged me in public speaking by assigning me speaking roles in drama class, glee club, and argumentation and debate class. Because I had a photographic memory, they gave me long pieces of poetry for recitation. They instructed me that it was the meter, rhythm, and rhyme of word phrases that I was keying into. When I left the stage, the stutter returned. Off stage, as I reverted to talking with classmates, they admonished me to, "Say it, don't spray it!" The kidding was relentless.

One night I was watching *The Tonight Show with Johnnie Carson*. This white dude named Mel Tillis stood to sing as smooth as silk. But as soon as he sat at the desk to converse with Carson, he stuttered and spat all over the man's suit! I thought, *Wow—that's me!*

CHAPTER SEVEN

The Batmobile and the Mack Truck

"I am blind, I can't see.
If I knock you down, don't you blame it on me!"

I RECALL REPEATING THIS RHYME when walking down the sidewalk with friends, arms linked together, usually three abreast. Perhaps I was the only one in the trio who kept his eyes completely closed. As we walked down the street, we thought people would jump out of the way when approached by three knuckleheads acting out a bit of childhood whimsy. Much later, I would discover that the other guys squinted to see approaching obstacles like trees and lampposts in our path.

One day I decided to play Blind Man's Bluff solo. As usual I closed my eyes tightly and did not squint to see where in the heck I was going. This was back in the day—I was seven years old—when Buicks, Studebakers, and Chevys were huge automobiles with dinner-plate headlights, rocket-like grilles, and sharp pointed tail lights. Some even had spaceship-styled fins along the side. Those cars seemed to us kids to be shaped like the Batmobile that Batman drove. In 1957, the new Chevy models sported exaggerated, sharp fish-fin tail lights. A seven-year-old kid in 1958, I had not spied one of those models parked near an empty lot where my friends and I were at play. By myself, I walked—eyes closed—right into the driver's side tail fin point. That really hurt! Falling backward and grabbing my head, I staggered a few steps. Seeing my disorientation, my friends rushed to pull my hands away from my face to see what I had done. My hand came away dripping with crimson blood.

Wailing in pain, I was whisked away by several friends who took me to my mom. After washing me up with a warm soapy washcloth, Mom again called a taxi and rushed me to the Emergency Room. The doctor looked down at me, perhaps remembering my Superman stunt a few years earlier, and shook his head. Then he opened a drawer, brought out a needle about three feet long to numb the skin around my forehead wound, before stitching it up. Eight stitches in my head! No more Blind Man's Bluff for me.

Returning to school the next morning, I hoped my large head bandage would at least be good for rare attention from the cute girl.

Much like the doctor, she just gazed into my eyes and shook her pigtails.

I have now developed a daily prayer ritual: "God, protect me from myself."

Even the boy, Arthur, was accident prone when under the tutelage of Merlin the Magician. Every time Arthur would have a narrow escape from injury, Merlin would affirm, "You are slowly learning to protect yourself from harm." Even in the twentieth century, I was slowly learning the same lessons as a kid.

As if parked vehicles were not hazardous enough, it wasn't long before I had a close encounter with a moving vehicle, and this was no family sedan! While safety filmstrips had warned me to look both ways before crossing a street, and to cross only at a designated crosswalk, those filmstrips were no match for the impetuosity of youth. Friendship—and the chance for an impromptu game of marbles—was more than a match for the fading memory of filmstrips administered like castor oil!

One day, when I was a second grader at Eugene Field Elementary School, I looked up during my morning walk to see a friend across the street. He was also on his way to school, and he held up a bag of new cat eye marbles, inviting me to play. Without giving it another thought, I suddenly bolted across the street ... without looking. Calling his name and swinging my brown paper lunch bag, I planned to use my skill to relieve him of his biggest, newest cat eye marble.

In mid-stride, I realized my ears were burning with the very loud sound of big-truck brakes. They were much nearer than seemed possible. It turned out that a dark green Mack truck was bearing down on me. Stopping on the tip toes of my sneakers at the deafening sound of the truck's brakes, I balanced on my toes. My brain told me that I had stopped just in time to feel the slightest touch of the truck bumper on my right thigh. Dust was everywhere, and the stench of burning brake pads and hydraulic fluid overwhelmed me.

Two red-faced men jumped from the truck's cab—one running to me around each end of the bumper of the truck—frantically shouting their worried question, "You okay, kid?!"

One man stared at me through fingerprinted glasses, clearly surprised that I was unhurt. The other, eyes wide under a sweaty forehead, held me with both hands checking to see if I had shattered something. They could not believe their good luck, at stopping before flattening a second-grader. Myself, I was pretty happy about it, too.

"You sure you're okay, son?" The first man repeated.

"You sure? We can call an ambulance," said the second man.

"No, I am fine," I said through a fog of disbelief. My brain was still processing the sounds and smells of the moment, unlike anything else I had ever experienced on a morning walk to school.

Dumbly, I studied the uniform of the man who still had not released my shoulders. ST. LOUIS SANITATION was embroidered over one pocket, red stitching on a well-used khaki shirt. Over the other pocket, ALVIN was embroidered in the same red thread.

A folded map, well-worn, covered the other man's name as it flowered out of his pocket. They both continued to stare me in the eyes. Then the one holding my shoulders slowly turned me around in circles to see again to make sure I was not bleeding, and nothing was broken.

"Are you sure you're okay son?" one of the men asked again. "We can call an ambulance."

"Yes, s … sir." I stammered, "I'm … f … fine."

Eventually, they walked gingerly back to their places in the truck, looking over their shoulders at me. Shocked, I was still standing in the middle of the street. Before they entered the truck, the driver said to me, "Go on over to the sidewalk now ... and watch out for traffic!"

"Yes sir, I wi wi wi ... will," I stuttered, walking carefully to the sidewalk.

Once back in their cab, the driver released the Mack's air brakes. Both men continued to stare at me, as if seeing a ghost. They would not, could not, get over the fact that I was not hurt, nor crying.

With knees knocking, and finally truly realizing what had just happened, or nearly happened, I turned with my friend and walked toward the school. He seemed more in shock than me, having seen the entire thing first hand. The marbles challenge had been forgotten.

Timing is everything. The science of the truck stopping at the precise moment that it did, and the gentle touch against my leg being the only sensation I felt, were things that I remember, even to this day. Oh, and I remember the marbles challenge, renewed at recess. By then, my nerves were fully awakened by my teacher's distress. She nearly fainted when she heard the story. Her anxiety compounded my own, which kept me from aiming with my usual finesse. My friend's largest cat eye marble, red and white swirled in a clear globe, remained safely within his canvas drawstring pouch.

Dad eventually lost his job at the Stix, Baer & Fuller Department Store. New, self-service elevators were installed, and he was given a pink slip. When I first heard about the pink slip, I wondered whether the department store had actually acted in bad enough taste to give my father, a man, a lady's slip—and a pink one, at that. But I knew enough to keep my silence in the muted atmosphere of the living room until it became clear to me that my dad had received a piece of pink paper with the bad news printed on it. Dad struggled with part-time work after that. He was unable to find work as an experienced elevator operator. His clothes became rattier, his forehead became deeply furrowed, and he had more time to discuss baseball with his friends. Most of the men on our street were in the same fix. When I returned from school in the afternoon, it wasn't unusual to see three or four dads sitting on the porch. They shared cigarettes and stories of botched innings, broken bats, baseball stats, and losing streaks.

One day when I returned from third grade, I found our furniture set out on the street. We moved a few blocks where Dad found another landlord who was a bit more indulgent. There, we lived in another first-floor flat through a few more St. Louis winters and a few more baseball seasons. Then one day when I returned from grade school, my brain newly focused on homework, I was again greeted by the sight of familiar furniture at the curb. I knew what it meant: a new landlord, a new apartment even more modest than the last, more space between the TV and the remaining chairs. Nomads were not just a bunch of folks on camels in the sandy Middle East.

CHAPTER EIGHT
The Ice Age

WHEN I WAS EIGHT years old, we moved from Enright Avenue a few blocks away to West Belle (then Evans Avenue) in North St. Louis. There I attended John Marshall Grade School. Our apartments consisted of a "shotgun" floor plan. It was said that if you fired a shotgun into the open front door, the shell would exit the kitchen door at the back of the house. There was a living room, two bedrooms down the hall, with a kitchen and bathroom in the back. Mom insisted on new linoleum in her kitchen because the old flooring was badly worn and crumbling at the edges. Somehow, she found the cash for a braided rug purchased at Stix, Baer & Fuller, where Daddy used to work. In the bathroom, the wallpaper was missing behind the toilet, and a cold draft rose from the basement through the uncovered wall, chilling your backside when you sat down. The toilet tank was cracked near the top so that you could always see the workings inside.

One winter, the floor furnace broke down and the temperature in the apartment fell into the low teens. We knew we were indoors because the snow was on the other side of the window. The landlord took his time getting the heater repaired. Before he got around to it, water pipes froze solid both in the kitchen and the bathroom. There was no running water anywhere in the apartment. Mom, demonstrating the resourcefulness of the Arkansas country woman she was, carried three galvanized buckets of water from the downstairs neighbor and heated them on the kitchen range. We three boys took turns bathing. All four burners plus the oven of the gas stove were constantly blazing all the while we were awake. We shuddered when we had to leave the warmth of the small heated kitchen. Standing in the bathtub—because it was too cold to sit down—we shuddered as Mom splashed hot water on our heads. We scrubbed ourselves vigorously with a big bar of Ivory soap. With the kitchen range providing the only heat in the apartment, and with very little insulation in the floors, walls or ceiling, the heat stopped about ten feet from the stove. We could see our breath condensation, right there in the house! For distraction, we played a game of blowing the steam and pretending we were dragons—or cigarette smokers.

Naturally, we spent most of our time in the tiny kitchen. If you needed anything from another room, you made a mad dash and returned as quickly as possible. There were no potty breaks in that house; that was simply out of the question. A stick of butter left on the table overnight was frozen in the morning. The same was true for a glass of milk or a sausage link. No need for a refrigerator, we turned it off and let the chill of winter keep everything cold.

Dad's Christmas gift for Mom, a glass jar of Pond's Cold Crème, froze in their bedroom, and nobody noticed until the heater was repaired two weeks later. By then, her dresser top had enjoyed a facial treatment.

Fortunately, the next door neighbors were friendly and considerate. They allowed us the privilege of fetching water from their bathtub and staying in the warmth of their living room for a couple hours each evening. Still, the reality was that we had to stop eating and drinking two hours before bedtime each evening so we would not have to bother them with restroom trips after they went to bed. We went to bed fully-clothed in shirt, sweater, pants, and socks. With three boys in one bed ramrod-straight, Mom spread covers four layers deep. She topped off our bedding with a special quilt, one of the few possessions which, before that, had been kept in a special box under her bed. If we three boys lay next to each other and kept our toes under the covers, we were warm enough to survive the night. On many evenings, I wrapped myself like a caterpillar in a cocoon and didn't unwrap until time to get up the next morning for school. When my turn came to wash up, Mom had the water heated on one of the stovetop burners. I spot bathed in record time and dressed so fast, it must have looked like Olympic tryouts.

During those lean times, our family spent many a winter night—sometimes for weeks and weeks on end—living in an apartment that was barely warmer than the snowstorm on the other side of the window. If Dad couldn't pay the gas bill, the company was not compassionate. They turned the gas off until he or Mom got enough work—perhaps a second job for her or a day job for Dad unloading pinball machines to confectioneries around St. Louis.

Playing these machines was a very popular activity before video arcades came into vogue. Most African-Americans were not able to land decent jobs from a GI Bill, and were relegated to the bottom rung of the working world. Most learned what it meant to be the last hired and first fired from any job, no matter how menial. Our family and thousands of others were left to a kind of Depression-era survival, even though the Depression was, to most of America, a distant memory.

CHAPTER NINE

Watch What You Think

I WAS NINE years old and had just seen the new movie *Hercules* starring Steve Reeves, no relation of George (Superman) Reeves. It was showing at the old St. Louis Theatre, now Powell Hall, home of the St. Louis Symphony Orchestra. I loved solitary play when I was a kid and never had a problem engaging my little imagination in the ritual. One day I found a six-foot wooden beam. It was splintered and half rotten, torn from an old abandoned house and left lying in the weeds along our alley. It was about four inches on each side. I grabbed it up and began hauling it over to my backyard to play Hercules. I'd read enough to know that Hercules was good at picking men up over his head and throwing them across a space to bounce off the opposite wall and then hit the floor with a SPLAT!

Now equipped with a beam of staggering weight—worthy of a youthful Hercules—I began to play the role. Pretending to stand in a Corinthian temple, and imagining the beam a worthy enemy, I would stand it up on end. With it tottering in place, towering six feet compared to my four-foot stature, I—"Hercules"—would confront the (strangely silent) evil-doer. A fight would break out, and "Hercules" would pick the man up over his head and throw him as far as he could. My plan called for me to throw the beam/enemy across the alley. However, the beam never flew very far since I was a skinny little kid with no muscle tone. I kept trying to stand the beam upright and grab hold of it, lift it and toss it. After a while, the beam would not stand up by itself anymore. I kept balancing it on end, but as soon as I backed away from it, the thing would topple over toward me. After about four or five attempts, I said to myself, "If this thing doesn't stand up and stay, God is a so and so!" (Actually, the name was much rougher, but you get the drift.) The very next time I put it in position and backed away—it stayed in place! *Great*, I thought, *it took me being rude and crude to the Creator for it to stay up.*

Turning around to compose myself in my Hercules character, I drew a deep breath and prepared for action. As soon as I turned back to face the beam, it was clear that the action had already begun. The tall beam was toppling toward me! It hit me squarely on the forehead, knocking me down. Stars of many colors were circling my head as my vision went blurry, and I fell to the ground. A large knot arose on my forehead. Crying loudly and holding my head, I sat up and stared at the beam lying motionless on the ground. Leaving that beam right there, I tottered to my feet and went to put ice on my head. Hercules had fled, and I was shaken to my core by immediate and righteous chastisement from Forces Unknown. My days as a Greek god were over; I decided not to harbor those thoughts again.

Later in my career, I was walking through a bookstore that housed rare books. As I love to say, "Sometimes I find books, and sometimes they find me." I felt an energy coming from one particular book on the third shelf from the top to my right. I turned and found that it was even protruding a bit from the other books on the shelf. When I took it down and opened it, the first thing that I saw was the name of the female author and copyright of 1902. The next time I turned the page it opened to this poem:

THOUGHTS

> You always can tell what your thoughts will do in
> bringing you hate or love;
> Because thoughts are things, and their airy wings
> are swift as a carrier dove;
> They follow the Law of the Universe
> that everything re-creates its kind;
> And they speed over the track, to bring you back,
> whatever went out from your mind.

It was at this point that I realized that quantum mechanics and physics are at the core of the construction of the universe. I also realized that mysticism and metaphysics are at the root of the Shaman's understanding: everything flows by the laws of yin-yang, alpha-omega, reap-sow, cause and effect. Premonition, intuition, precognition, clairvoyance, déjà vu, auto-suggestion, and ESP, all the result of the energy emanating from one's mind in the form of "thought."

CHAPTER TEN

Flash Flood in Cuivre River State Park

WHEN I WAS TEN years old, I went to summer camp for two weeks in Troy, Missouri. It was called Camp Sherwood Forest in Cuivre River State Park. One day we went on a hike into the forest to camp overnight. We stomped through the woods joyously singing camp songs,

"The ants go marching one by one, Hoorah, hoorah!"

"Goodbye Old Paint, I'm leaving Cheyenne,"

"There's a hole in the bucket Dear Liza Dear Liza,"

"They built the ship Titanic and when they were through, they thought they had a ship that the water wouldn't go through. ..."

When we arrived at our campsite, we found that the camp office had already sent a Jeep out to deliver our tents, food, and firewood. What a delight to see all our camping supplies ready for us to use when we arrived!

As we were pitching our tents, a hard rain came. The sky began to fill with purple/gray cumulus clouds. The day turned to night as threatening clouds that looked like alligator scales filled the skies. Our counselor looked visibly shaken by the quick turn of events. He stared upward for several minutes, and I saw his face turn very serious. His usual jovial manner changed to alarm. He ordered us to stop what we were doing and take shelter; water was coming in torrents! The sky just opened up, soaking the ground in no time. Our tents, pitched on the now-soaked meadow, began to fill up with water themselves. Muddy water was soon ankle-deep, inside the tents.

Deafening thunder resounded without intermission. BOOM!BOOM!BOOM!BOOM!BOOM!BOOM!

Branch lightning filled the skies as electric currents raced one another to create new circuits from cloud to cloud to treetop to ground. When we dared to open our eyes, it looked as if the heavens were mad at us.

We took immediate shelter—if you could call it that. Our fair-weather plastic and canvas tent was flapping in the wind, poles shaking in our hands (surely the tent stakes would not hold in this mud) and the rain was coming inside like a communal shower. We were at the mercy of the elements. Since these were small, two-man tents, each of us was isolated at one end of a very small fabric shelter, unable to see how others were faring in the deluge. My buddy and I were huddled in terror as the wind whipped our tent like a bit of crepe paper caught in a ceiling fan. With a relentless howling wind filling our ears, it sounded like the end of the world.

After an hour of thunder, lightning, and drenching downpour, the skies finally cleared. Our counselor, a tall white college student named Bob Heisler, was as alarmed as we had been by the sudden storm. Very attentive to us and dedicated to our safety, Bob organized a clean-up and soothed our shaken spirits. Then, he set about organizing a much drier campsite. When we were confident that our tents were recovering from their earlier soaking, Bob lead us on an exploratory hike. Seeing him take charge was a relief, and we were soon ready to follow him into the brush.

Now it was time to explore the bluffs and descend to the bottom of the switchback trail to a "dry" creek bed below, where an old corn silo stood. Eight boys were eager to explore, and then there was me. I was suffering. My tummy was hurting because I ate something for breakfast that did not agree with me. The real culprit, however, was way too much bug juice. Bug Juice was our name for an over-sweetened flavoring that we added to water. It came in slim packets like the well-known soda pop alternative, but it was the bargain basement knock-off of the name brand product. We campers called it Bug Juice because of its uncanny ability to attract bugs of all species, seemingly within a four-mile radius. Our Bug Juice was labeled Cherry Red. The food coloring tasted very cherry, and indeed it looked quite red! It was laden with lots of sugar, and it was unrefrigerated on that summer afternoon as we hiked uphill and down. We did not know if it was the red color or the aroma of liquid sugar that attracted insects of every shape and description. There was no cover for the jar when we lifted it overhead to drink from the communal batch. With every hefting of the jug and neck-craning, lifting to drink, several dozen more of Missouri's finest insects would dive in, kamikaze-style. If not swallowed instantly, they would die in the concoction, probably more from a sugar overdose than drowning. The stress of experiencing a terrifying storm so intimately, followed by drinking in so much sugar-water, laden with so much coloring, on top of a large breakfast probably led to my illness. Until the nausea and diarrhea subsided, I was able to convince the counselor that I should stay at the campsite while he took the other seven down the one-hundred-foot-tall bluffs to see the corn silo. After a while, my tummy ache went away, and I was feeling lonely. I thought, *I can't believe I'm the only one up here in this stupid campsite while everybody else is having fun at the bottom of the bluff.* I got up and ambled down the trail, which was well-defined and featured beautiful overlooks. I soon felt a calm, a sense of oneness with the natural world. It was my first experience of observing a violent storm and its peaceful aftermath from the point-of-view of a camper. My quiet solo trek in the stillness that followed the storm was my first experience of nature's return to calm. It was fabulous!

When I got to the middle of the "dry" creek bed, I stopped. Ahead, I saw my friends and the counselor exploring around the corn silo. As I stood there, my "spider senses" started tingling like Spiderman! I hesitated to move any further toward the corn silo. I was aware of hearing what I thought was an old truck with a busted muffler coming around the bend of the creek about 300 yards behind me. I stood immobile, my eyes fixed on the bend, waiting to see the raggedy old truck come into view, all the while wondering how it got down the bluff. What I saw was a sudden wall of roiling water several feet taller than me—coming straight at me! The wall of water rushed in to reclaim the dry riverbed!

Some reservoir must have broken during the storm. Now here I was, standing in the middle of a dry tributary of The Cuivre River, which wasn't going to be dry for much longer. My instincts immediately made me run to higher ground. Without making a conscious decision, I found myself rushing back toward the bluff. By the time I ran up the trail a safe distance from the creek, the rolling, crashing water came rushing just below me. *Just* below me! I saw logs, rocks, mud, trash cans and trash go by as the creek bed filled with the new current. Several snakes of various lengths swam the torrent, seeking higher ground just as I had.

When the rest of the group came to see what the noise was, they all froze in horror—on the opposite bank. The look on their faces was easy to read: *where did this river come from and, more importantly, how do we get back to the bluff trail?* Over the roar of the current, I yelled and waved my arms until the counselor saw me. He told me to stay where I was. Well, duh!

After an hour or so our counselor decided the current had slowed down enough, that it might be safe to cross. He told the campers to wait until he went into the middle of the creek to see how deep and how strong it was. When he realized it was only up to his chest, he went back, and they all had a conference. A life and death conference, I am certain. He had the campers link their hands and slowly inch their way into the creek. As I passively watched from my dry, comfortable perch, they slowly crept across the creek to safety. As we slowly ambled our way back up the bluff to the campsite, everyone was completely quiet. The whole experience they had was, to me, like watching a television show.

During camp dinner that evening, there was plenty to talk about. We had actually forgotten—temporarily—our encounter with nature when the dark, clear sky revealed a celestial spiral known as the Milky Way. "That's the galaxy we are a part of," our counselor told us as we lay on our backs. "It looks like a long strip of a pale white cloud, stretching from horizon to horizon. Actually, it is billions and billions of stars, galaxies and exploding thermonuclear suns, all spiraling from left to right," our counselor exclaimed. Looking upward in amazement, we realized that each of us was simply a passenger on a ride through the Universe!

As I looked into infinite space, I realized how fortunate I was, witnessing and watching the cosmos so passively in relation to the flash flood hours earlier. A feeling of profound peace overtook me as I slipped into a restful sleep—all my camp buddies and counselor safe and sound. In twelve hours, we went from experiencing nature in one of her most dynamic and powerful moments to a time of safety in the peace and awe of the cosmos. That night was my first awakening to the meaning of being part of a Universal Plan and finding my purpose as a part of the "infinite scheme of things."

Whatever my purpose was to be, I knew it would have to be met with patience, confidence, and courage.

CHAPTER ELEVEN

Tear the Roof Off the Sucker

WHEN I WAS FIFTEEN years old, we had a bad storm one night, and the roof over our back porch was badly damaged. One support beam that held the roof over the entire back porch had split, causing the roof to sag in a deep arc under the weight of wood, roof tile, and water. The landlord was very slow to initiate repairs. In the interim, because the unsupported roof presented a danger to Mom, Dad, and the three of us boys, we were admonished to refrain from using the back door. If we wanted to play in the back yard, we had to go out the front door and go around the gangway.

I was accustomed to going through the kitchen door to the backyard and did not want to change my routine. Walking all the way around the house seemed an inconvenience. I decided to take matters into my own hands, literally.

One night I decided to orchestrate a clandestine operation. Using a thirty-foot clothesline found in the basement storage area, I secretly tied the rope to the one remaining support beam. Mom was in the kitchen where saucepans were huffing, and the percolator was singing. I decided to be very careful and not to be in the vicinity when "it all went down." Walking casually toward the back fence, I timed the operation with precision. After several moments of gathering courage, I pulled the rope! The support beam cantered away from the house and the porch roof came crashing down! The sound of the implosion was tremendous! Falling back on my behind, as I watched roofing tiles smash into the backyard, I saw Mom in the kitchen window. She jumped! She screamed!

I thought to myself, *time to go!*

Running around through a neighbor's backyard, I slowed as our front porch came into view. Taking pains to slow my breathing, I entered our front door and scraped my shoes. Pretending I heard a noise from my room, I sauntered into the kitchen without speaking a word. My mom was looking out the back door now. When she turned to see me, an expression of relief shone on her face. She said, "It's a blessing you weren't out there when it fell!"

I remained silent. Mom, so accustomed to dirt on the seat of my pants, never wondered why I had landed on my bottom. Someone's conscience was stoked that night, but not mine. The landlord was so embarrassed, that he immediately called a wrecking crew to haul the debris away and rebuild a safe back porch. We even got a new kitchen linoleum, too! I will never forget the floral pattern of that new kitchen floor. It was the very pattern of guilt.

As I watched them follow up on my good handiwork the next day, I thought about two movies I had seen when I was much younger. In one, Hercules pulled a temple down with chains. In another, the super-human Samson pushed down a temple full of Philistines. Steve Reeves played Hercules and Victor Mature played Samson. Oh, yeah, I played the role of the Night Rambler! The secret of my operation remained just that until now. Hey, my intuition told me if we had kept that porch like it was, someone was bound to get hurt or worse, so I lost no sleep over the "smooth move."

CHAPTER TWELVE

The Marvel Comics Group

*The comics that shaped my imagination and
introduced me to fantasy and the Hero's Journey*

WHEN I GREW UP in North St. Louis, the most popular sport was boxing. Not so much because it was competition, but more because it was a way of survival. Recreation centers like Tandy, Gamble, Wohls, Capre, Desoto, Vashon, Buder, and Yalem specialized in training young black boys for boxing competitions. The bigger motive to a black youth, however, was to protect yourself from bullies and to defend your honor when challenged, which was sure to happen on the streets of Saint Louis in those days.

In the 1960s, gangs were in full force in North St. Louis, not for the purpose of selling drugs, but merely to defend turf. In the Ville, the area surrounding Sumner High School, there was the Taylor and Cottage Gang (the TCs). Around Beaumont High School nearby, the arch rival of the TCs, the Vanderventer Bugs held the turf. The Bugs later changed their name to the Vanderventer Strips. Boxing, wrestling, and knife fighting were the ways of the streets. I never took an interest in the boxing phenomenon because I discovered the Marvel Comics Group between 1961 and 1966.

While visiting the neighborhood five-and-dime store and pharmacy, I saw this eye-catching collection of superhero comic books.

They were on a rack on the wall behind the counter with a special track light on them to illuminate the superior artwork. When I asked to see the newest issues, the clerk was happy to show me each one. I bought them all: *The Fantastic Four, The Amazing Spiderman, The Mighty Thor, Daredevil, The Hulk, The Avengers, Iron Man, The X Men, Ant Man, The Wasp* and *Captain America!* This series of comics shaped my imagination and introduced me to fantasy and the Hero's Journey.

Unlike Superman, who had no flaws—except that little problem of being exposed to Kryptonite—the Marvel Comics' characters all had various personality flaws. Their flaws made for excellent subplots in the monthly stories of their lives. With the excellent writing of Stan Lee and the masterful drawings of Jack (King) Kirby, I was transported to realms that were far beyond the ghettos of North St. Louis. My passion for reading took a quantum leap as I became interested in science, mythology, storytelling, and adventure.

While others were at the boxing and recreation centers, I read and collected Marvel Comics. Now to be clear, I was no "couch potato kid." I loved corkball, a game that involved an old broom or mop stick and a tennis ball. It was a game for two or more players. When you, the batter, had three strikes, the pitcher got to bat. If you were in the outfield and successfully caught three ground balls in your glove, you got to bat. There was no running of bases.

Mumbly Peg was exciting, too. With an ice pick, we chopped a patch of dirt up into a "mush" so the ice pick would stand in the dirt. Then, each one had to flip the ice pick in different ways until it—eventually—landed point down and stuck in the dirt, handle up.

I loved playing marbles. I was the marble king. That's *marble,* not "Marvel," in this case. I played marbles nearly every day, eventually collecting two dresser drawers full. My favorites were the "cat eyes"—combinations of blue, gray, green, purple, and yellow swirls in clear plastic spheres. When they caught the light, they lit up like the eyes of a cat. We also built "boxcars" out of old crates and scrap wood, and raced them in the alley. When the wheels fell off, we made bows and arrows with strips of wood and any twine we could find behind the neighborhood grocery. Hand-me-down roller skates—the kind that we had to clamp onto our shoes—were a favorite for several years, but gave way to bicycles.

During the roller skate years, we also played dodge ball and tag. When we played hide and seek, we chanted, "Last night, night before, twenty-four robbers at my door. I got up, let 'em in, hit 'em in the head with a rolling pin."

Then came the challenge, "All hid?"

If someone said no, we repeated the chant. When no one answered (meaning that everyone was hidden), the search began. If you found someone, you had to race to the tree to touch it. If one of the hidden players was seen, he or she had to reach the "home" tree before the searcher or else they became the next searcher.

I was always involved in creative play. We kids used our imaginations to make up games and so doing, we expanded the use of our growing brains. We had no idea that what we were doing was, in a way, educational. We were simply playing as expected. I hear from many educators today that, because of excessive use of video games and computers, kids are losing this crucial faculty of their brain.

In my quiet times back then, I read Marvel Comics and ended up collecting comics dated from 1960 to 1968. I stopped buying them in my sophomore year of high school when I became "too cool" to read comics. After all, at the advanced age of sixteen, self-image is everything. I joined the high school gymnastics team and became quite proficient on the mats and parallel bars. I loved the forward roll, jack-knife, back-roll and hand stand. In my senior year, I became a second-string football player, a fullback. My real motivation to play football was the coveted letter sweater. Self-image, again. Sumner's letter sweater was maroon and white, the school colors, with a huge S (like Superman) on the front. After graduation, I handed that hard-won sweater to some girl. I never saw the sweater or the girl again.

The comic books I still have. I learned to put them in acid-free plastic bags with cardboard backing and place them in a long box. When the *Avengers* movie trailers came out, an auction company in St. Louis hosted a comic convention in St. Louis County. I asked one of the auctioneers to come to my house and examine my collection. He took my *Avengers #1* copy to Florida for appraisal by the CGC, the comic grading company. They appraised it at a 6.0 condition, enough to earn me $2,000 at the comic convention. I thought, not a bad investment for the dime I shelled out for it in 1963! I could not part with the other comics, however. I still treat them the way a curator handles rare books at the Library of Congress.

CHAPTER THIRTEEN

April 4, 1968

I WAS AT MY MARTIAL ARTS CLASS at 6 p.m. on April 4, 1968, doing my *katas* in the white belt class in South St. Louis. The first I knew anything was wrong was when a white male instructor who was a black belt came over to ask me, "Are they rioting in the Negro community right now?"

Confused, I asked him "Why would there be rioting in the Negro area?"

He said, "Haven't you heard? Somebody killed Martin Luther King Jr. in Memphis, Tennessee, today! They think it was a white guy, but he got away." I was stunned.

"They killed Dr. King today?"

"Yeah," he said. "It's all over the news."

I bowed out at the dojo and told my Sensei, Sam Brock, that I needed to leave early. After dressing in street clothes, I caught the two busses back home. St. Louis at this time was extremely segregated. Ninety-nine percent of whites lived in South St. Louis, and ninety-nine percent of blacks lived in North St. Louis. There were no karate schools in North St. Louis, so I took the trip across town twice a week to study the martial arts.

En route home, I was amazed at how I was told this information. A black guy with a white belt and *gi*, I was told by a white guy with a black belt and gi. Somehow, that aggregation of opposites seemed symbolic, even significant. It seemed a clever and somehow universal example of The Law of Opposites to me. On the bus ride, I went back in my mind to where I was when I heard that President John F. Kennedy was assassinated. At 1:30 p.m. on the afternoon of November 22, 1963, I had been in the sixth-grade art class at Turner Middle School in St. Louis, struggling to manage the serpentine flow of dark watercolors on rough paper.

When I arrived home, my family had the TV on, watching network news. In that time, there was no cable TV, and broadcast news was dominated by CBS, ABC and NBC network news. All the talk on all three networks was of the King murder and the rioting that had erupted in many major cities. Burning buildings and looting were being televised live from coast to coast. The police and National

Guard were on alert to arrest any rioters and, in some cities, to shoot looters on sight. St. Louis was the only major city without rioting or looting.

Later, during the international manhunt, Scotland Yard and the British Secret Service made an arrest at Heathrow Airport in London. Scotland Yard took James Earl Ray into custody for shooting Dr. King. Ray claimed he had help, but no other suspects were charged. Investigations later traced money found in Ray's possession at the time of his capture back to a "financier" in St. Louis, Missouri—where no rioting occurred. Ray later recanted his complicity in the assassination, saying a person named "Rauel" was his contact in the plot, and he (Ray) was not the triggerman.

FBI Director J. Edgar Hoover was adamant about not diligently seeking possible co-conspirators and thought that the civil rights movement was communist-inspired. He also made no attempt to hide his dislike for the civil rights leader, calling Dr. King "one of the most dangerous people in America" and "a threat to Democracy."

I was still much too young to process all of the bewildering developments in American political, social, and racial scenes at the time. However, I had been intensely interested in current events ever since President Kennedy (JFK) had threatened Russia and Cuba with nuclear war in 1961. Though still too young to understand everything I witnessed, I was fascinated by events unfolding on television throughout the 1960s and after. The Cuban Missile Crisis presented an apparent international intrigue that had much of America, and certainly me, on the edges of our sofas in front of the evening TV news.

Current events were not the only tempting dramas of those years. Sean Connery had burst onto the movie screen as "Bond—James Bond" in *Doctor No* and *Goldfinger*. Efrem Zimbalist Jr. portrayed an intrepid detective with nerves of steel on the weekly television series *The FBI*. It was a heady time for a boy growing into manhood, a time when the country was reluctantly leaving the comfort and security of the 1950s behind. We were unwittingly headed toward the 1970s, which would bring an energy crisis, the *de facto* loss of a war in Vietnam, collapse of hundreds of savings and loan institutions, and the resignation of President Richard Nixon. As a young teen during the 1960s, I grew to social and political awareness during an unsettled time. It was a time that would demand definition not only by politicians and other established leaders, but also by young people like myself, who were just then coming of age.

Little did I know how all these events would shape my career ambitions by the time I became a senior in high school. My education was only beginning.

One of the main things that saved America from descending into total madness in the 1960s was the music. Our consciousness was treated to Motown greats such as the Temptations, the Four Tops, Gladys Knight & the Pips, Stevie Wonder, Marvin Gaye, Smokey Robinson & and the Miracles, and the Supremes! Some folks who did not know better actually thought Martha & the Vandellas' "Dancin' in the Street" was intended to incite rioting! Motown execs and Martha Reeves said, "No, it was an R&B song about happily dancing in the street!"

There was indeed a message in the music of Peter, Paul and Mary, who struck a deep spiritual chord in America with meaningful lyrics and smooth harmonies. Pete Seeger was another icon who healed and inspired people with original though folkish songs like "We Shall Overcome," "Where Have All the Flowers Gone?" and "Little Boxes." Bob Dylan—"The Times They Are A-Changin'" and "Subterranean Homesick Blues," (1962)—was perhaps the most outspoken singer-songwriter of the day. His influence touches us still.

A powerful group called TSOP—The Sound of Philadelphia—came on the scene and contributed to my formidable collection of 45s and 33-1/3 vinyl records. The O Jays, under the direction of Gamble & Huff, made some incredible music that resonated with how we as a nation were doing in the late '60s and early '70s. One line in an O Jays song says, "Music is the Healing Force of the world ... misunderstood by every man, woman, boy, and girl. ..."

People always talk about the San Andreas earthquake fault running through California, but there is a very active fault running from New Madrid in southern Missouri up toward St. Louis. The New Madrid Fault is centered in the *bootheel* of Missouri (it looks like a boot heel when you look at it on a map).

One Saturday morning in 1968, my dad and I were the only ones home. He was in his room in bed and I was in my bed just two rooms away. I had just awakened and was slowly becoming aware of my surroundings when the room started wobbling like a giant vat of gelatin! I grabbed my covers and watched in awe as the walls, ceiling, floor, and furniture started gyrating and moving in unison with a low rumble. My dad yelled from his room, "Bobby! What are you doing in there?" That house was wobbling like crazy, and he was blaming it on me!

I guess he thought I was playing with my imaginary chemistry set. I yelled back, "It's not me, it must be an earthquake!" After about eighteen seconds it subsided, and all was normal.

Luckily there was no damage to the house when he and I inspected it. There was minimal damage citywide, but it certainly got everyone's attention! That quake reminded St. Louis residents that there is an active seismic fault under Missouri soil!

The *real* "rumblings" would soon come to America, however, and from a very different kind of energy.

Even though my favorite sport was gymnastics, I wanted a letter sweater in varsity football. When I tried out for the team and made third-string fullback, the thrill was palpable. At 160 pounds, I was about twenty pounds lighter than the first- and second-string fullbacks, but—*hey*—I was on the team! With an almost reverential pride, I wore the white sweater with the huge maroon S stitched across the chest. The real reason for the sweater was the theory that it turned a regular guy into a "babe magnet."

Maybe.

It would have worked had I not been so shy! Buffed from gymnastics workouts and training, I looked good in the buff. At one football practice, however, a realization put me off my game. The coach had us scrimmage two at a time, putting the football between the two facing players. On the whistle, one was to grab the ball and ram into the other. When my turn came, I took my position and waited. On the whistle, my opponent grabbed the ball and lunged for me. I remember rising slightly and—miraculously—stopping him in his tracks using my washboard solar plexus muscles! My teammates were duly impressed. "Way to go, Norfolk! All right! Whoo hoo!"

The coached yelled, "No, no that's not the way to do it!" He called out to two of his first-string guys, "Show them how it done!" The two bruisers assumed the position. On the whistle, one guy scooped up the ball, and then both brutes rammed their helmets into one another. A sickening crunching sound filled the air as they collapsed onto the ground, shuddering. After a moment, the two gladiators staggered to their feet, obviously pretending it didn't hurt. The coach spat an orgasmic sigh of relief. "Now that's how it's done!"

I thought to myself "Hell, no!" I will never subject my brain and spinal system to such abuse. After that, I purposely did it "wrong" at each scrimmage. I would rather stay third string than turn my spine into a human Slinky! I would never do that to myself. The history of brain and spine injuries that have dominated college and professional football is a testament to the perils of gladiator sports which have taken on an almost religious fervor. If you miss church to go to The Game, presumably God will understand!

CHAPTER FOURTEEN
Memories of Sumner High School

WHEN I ATTENDED Charles Sumner High School in St. Louis, Missouri, I was familiar with only a few African-American leaders. Among them were Dr. Martin Luther King Jr.; Ralph Bunche, the 1950 Nobel Peace Prize winner; Medgar Evers, the Mississippi voting rights organizer; Ralph Abernathy, co-founder of the Southern Christian Leadership Conference; Adam Clayton Powell Jr., the congressman from New York City; Fannie Lou Hamer, co-founder of the Mississippi Freedom Democratic Party; Marion Anderson, the first African-American to perform with the New York Metropolitan Opera (in 1955); Jesse Jackson, the future "shadow senator" from Washington, D.C.; and the founder the Tuskegee Normal and Industrial Institute (now known as Tuskegee University), and Booker T. Washington.

My school was named for Charles Sumner, a white abolitionist senator from Massachusetts. Before the U. S Civil War, Sumner made the error of saying something negative about South Carolina Senator

Andrew Butler's love of the institution of slavery in America. Rep. Preston Brooks, a nephew of Butler, was intent on exacting revenge for his "maligned uncle." Brooks brought a bamboo cane onto the Senate floor and beat Senator Sumner senseless. Brooks pummeled "The good senator from Massachusetts" until the cane broke.

Sumner, bleeding from the head, was sent on extended leave to recover from the vicious attack. Brooks got off by paying a fine of $300. Meanwhile, dozens of canes, each bearing the inscription, "Hit him again!", were sent to Brooks from Southern slave sympathizers.

Sumner High School was later built to honor Senator Sumner. It is considered the oldest high school for blacks west of the Mississippi River. Luminaries who have attended include comedian and political satirist Dick Gregory, Soul Singer Tina Turner, Ron Townsend of the pop group The Fifth Dimension, R&B icon Chuck Berry, comedian Redd Foxx, tennis star Arthur Ashe, and mezzo-soprano Grace Bumbry.

It was at Sumner High that my creativity was honed, beginning in the tenth grade. Our drama teacher, Claire Lockman Boyce, and music teachers, Ora Byrd Taylor and Kenneth Brown Billups, put me in poetry recitals, Glee Club, and plays. My first recital was as a ten-year-old kid when I memorized Jimmy Dean's "Big Bad John." Today I use a satirical line that people think Rap and Hip Hop started in the 1980s in the black community, but Dean, a country white boy, seemed to have hit on it in 1961!

In high school, I was Augie, the race jockey, in *Saint Louis' Woman*. I imitated comedian "Pigmeat" Markham in a rendition of "Here Come De Judge," and copied the voice of Melvin Franklin, bass singer of The Temptations, in the song "Old Man River" in the Senior Spectacular at Charles Sumner High School. Mrs. Taylor even had me sing lead in The Kingston Trio song, "Tom Dooley." When

I hit that last note, "Poor boy you're bound to die!" the girls in the audience erupted in squeals and applause. A slight stutter that I had from childhood made me bashful and shy. In time—with a combination of meter, rhythm, rhyme, humor, and pathos—the speech impediment eventually disappeared. Neither my teachers nor I had any idea where it went.

My tenth-grade drama teacher at Charles Sumner High School, Claire Lockman (Boyce), recommended I study relaxation techniques, which brought me to transcendental meditation. The Beatles went to India and studied under the Maharishi Mahesh Yogi. Their journey drew the attention of an entire generation to Transcendental Meditation. "TM" quickly became a craze. When I found a TM studio, the fee to learn the art was beyond my means. With encouragement from teachers, I decided to check out TM at the St. Louis Public Library. I walked out with seven books on the subject!

Through a combination of self-directed reading, performance, and meditation, my stuttering eventually stopped. Later in life, I read news reports about other people who overcame speech problems. They included people I admired: Maya Angelou, Oprah Winfrey, James Earl Jones, country singer Mel Tillis and Bruce Willis. It turned out that, like me, they had overcome their speech impediments through performance art and public speaking.

My other favorite teachers were Louis McKinney (my gymnastics coach and science teacher) and Beatrice Cooper Bell, a short, brilliant woman who was not afraid to pummel her eighth-grade boys when they misbehaved. I was wise enough not to cross her. Counselors who made a difference for me in high school were Tanzie Mayer, Rick Reynolds, Mikki Brewster, Ida Goodwin Woolfolk, Papa Jack, Mr. Washington, Mr. (Doon) Miller, and Mr. Algee.

My own personal Hall of Shame for teachers would include a sixth-grade teacher who made me do fifty deep knee bends for every minute I was late for school. I was not an early riser and had problems being slow in the mornings. She also whipped me with a rattan, a yard-long dowel rod wrapped with black electricians tape. This corporal punishment was meted out because I did not learn my multiplication tables fast enough for her satisfaction. Corporal punishment was common in St. Louis Public Schools in the 1960s. The practice eventually ended with lawsuits, child-abuse laws, and parent-teacher brawls on school property!

CHAPTER FIFTEEN

Ambushed at Dinner

ONE DAY DURING MY FRESHMAN YEAR in high school, I was walking back home from Sherman Park Playground on Kingshighway Avenue. About a mile from my house, there are some great mounds with a quarter-mile track at the top. I liked to run the track and run up and down the mounds. That day, I stopped by a Chinese takeout place on Easton Avenue (now MLK Drive) and picked up a dinner to eat on the way home. Slowly continuing my walk and enjoying pork fried rice while window shopping, I found myself about three blocks from home in The Ville when an unmarked police car pulled up beside me with two white detectives in it. The detective on the passenger side yelled out of the open window, "Hey you, boy—get in the back of the car now!"

Startled and terrified, I immediately obeyed. As I sat down, the cop that ordered me into the car turned in an accusatory posture and said "What were you doing, looking in those store windows?"

I replied, "Err, window shopping."

"Yeah right!" he replied.

Then the driver scowled at me through the rearview mirror and said "You aren't in any trouble, are you?"

I said, "No, sir. I'm not in any trouble."

"You been out here stealing?"

"No, sir."

The passenger cop asked, "What's your name?"

I told him, and he said, "We will see about that!" He then called dispatch on the car radio, gave them my name and said to look for a rap sheet on me. An eternity passed as finally the dispatcher said "No record on a Robert Lee Norfolk—over?"

With a look of slight disappointment the cop replied, "Copy that, over and out." He then turned back to me and spat out: "Oh I see you haven't been caught yet! Get out of the car!" I got out and went back on the sidewalk, trembling. I walked down Easton Avenue, watching as the police car pulled away and sped down the street. An event like that is hard to forget. The message to me was that *the government had sent armed officers out into the streets under the assumption that young men who looked like me were the enemy.* Even in these evolved modern times, experiences such as I had that day continue to happen too often. Some people in America know that reality all too well. Others can only imagine that it still happens. This dehumanizing behavior is happening thousands of times every week, all across our country.

My high school graduation with the Class of 1969 was as grand an event as possible for a predominantly black school at the time. The teachers planned field trips to Forest Park for picnics and visits to the zoo. The more socially inclined teachers created a series of informal sock hops and a formal dance. Every teacher held a party in their classroom. The best one was hosted by drama teacher Claire Lockman (Boyce), who was only four years older than we seniors but infinitely wiser.

While I was amazed at the prospect of graduation, figuring out what I was to do with the rest of my life was a conundrum. I was determined to go to college. The characters who populated movies based on Ian Fleming's novels dominated my thoughts. In my dreams—both day and night—I imagined that I *was* James Bond—007. I wanted to move up in the economic ladder and go to college. Sean Connery, who portrayed James Bond in *Goldfinger*, was the reason. I applied for a job as a page at the Justice Department, the Central Intelligence Agency, and the FBI. I sought scholarships at Howard University and George Washington University, institutions that seemed worthy of Agent 007.

As one destined to replace James Bond in the popular imagination (or at least in a clandestine role), my intention was to serve my country and be a federal official. Turned down by Howard and Washington Universities, schools that clearly did not channel my unexpressed vision to serve my country and save the world, I enrolled at Forest Park Community College (FPCC) in St. Louis. During my time at FPCC, I experienced a sudden and jarring awakening about the political climate in America.

CHAPTER SIXTEEN
Fish Eye, Politics, and Malcolm X

"It was his eye—yes it was this! He had the eye
of a vulture—a pale blue eye with a film over it.
Whenever it fell upon me, my blood ran cold."
—From *The Tell-Tale Heart* by Edgar
Allen Poe

THE TRANSITION FROM CARNIVORE TO VEGETARIAN was dramatic and sudden. I had studied the concept from 1975-76 but loved to visit the seafood and fish shops for lunch and dinner. After all, I was a Pisces, and it seemed natural. One day while working at the Arch, I got the "brilliant idea" to go to Soulard Farmers Market two miles from where I worked to buy a whole catfish to cook for dinner. I never had field dressed, beheaded, gutted, scaled, and butchered a fish for eating before, but by golly I was going to do it this particular evening. After I had left the Arch, I drove to Soulard and went to the fish house area. There a farmer had just come back with his fresh catch of the day. Catfish and buffalo fish were spread out on ice inside the display case. These huge animals still twitched with life. The one I was interested in was about twenty pounds. Its mouth was still moving as it lay on the ice. I gazed at the fish sucking at the air, slowly suffocating as its gills methodically opened and closed.

"I'll take that one," I exclaimed to the farmer.

He lifted the gasping fish from the ice and asked me if I wanted him to cut it up and prepare it for me to take home.

"No, that's all right," I said, "I'll butcher it at home."

He wrapped the fish up in newspaper and I made the purchase. I dropped it into the back seat and drove home. When I arrived at the apartment, it was early evening. My wife and young son were at relatives visiting. I unwrapped the newspaper and found the catfish still alive, but just barely. Laying it on the kitchen countertop by the sink, I made ready to "prepare dinner."

Swiveling in the galley kitchen to reach the butcher knife and cleaver from their drawer, I turned back to the fish to begin the gutting. The Venetian blinds were angled so that the evening sun rays poured into the kitchen. A warm ray of the evening light hit the eye of the fish, making it glow with an eerie sparkle. The effect of that dramatic lighting was such that I suddenly fell back against the cabinet, dropping the knives. My eyes were locked on that prehistoric looking fish, its scales as suited to a reptilian monster as to my family's dinner. Time stood still. I was unable to move as I watched the upturned eye of this catfish glowing at me. My mind went to the times I played marbles as a kid, to my favorite cat eyes. This eye looked just like my marbles, but the mouth of the fish was still slowly moving.

I watched until the sunlight changed outside, and the rays moved away from the eye, so that it went dim. The mouth was now still. I gathered up the knives from the floor, dropped them in the dishwater, and wrapped the fish back up in the newspaper. Hurriedly, I took it to the dumpster out back and deposited it. My vegetarian diet was officially launched at that moment.

I later found out something very elemental. The cells in our body need the nutrients and vitality found in foods. The healthier the food, the better to combust into energy. This is the basis of the acid-alkaline balance in our body's cells. Everything we consume leaves an ash. Alkaline substances are converted into pure energy. Acids collect in various parts of the body. Eventually, the microbes in the cells are worn down by the collected acids and diseases of various kinds are the result. So I concluded that when we say someone died of "natural causes," the "causes" were perpetuated with fork and spoon. This knowledge carried over to white sugar, white flour, processed foods, and foods contaminated with pesticides, herbicides, mercury, and arsenic.

An Elder once told me, "Bobby, everything that's good to you, isn't always good for you."

I had been unable to assemble the pieces of the jigsaw puzzle that was American politics, including the social upheaval taking place around the war in Vietnam and race relations. I knew that Dr. King had been murdered. I was aware of desegregation dramas playing out in Selma, Alabama, and Oxford, Mississippi, and elsewhere. But, in my four years of high school I had never heard of Malcolm X, one of the most influential people in America. Malcolm X was a national spokesman for the Honorable Elijah Muhammad of the Nation of Islam. When JFK was assassinated in Dallas, Texas, November 22, 1963, Malcolm X told the press, "It was a case of the chickens coming home to roost." By his metaphor, he meant that the government had created a climate of cause and effect through policies that held people down, inciting anger that quite naturally sought an outlet.

Elijah Muhammad suspended Malcolm X for the comment because so many loved and adored President Kennedy. Malcolm X later traveled to Mecca in Saudi Arabia and found out Muslims are of many colors, races, and nationalities. When he returned to the United States, he renounced the idea that whites were "blue-eyed devils." He was immediately discharged from the Nation of Islam. Not one to be held down or pushed to the side, Malcolm X formed his own organization, The Organization of Afro-American Unity, in 1965. Shortly afterward, Malcolm X was assassinated in the Audubon Ballroom in New York's Harlem.

In my freshman year of college, *The Autobiography of Malcolm X* was required reading in English Literature class. Alex Haley, then famous for his bestselling book of the African-American experience, *Roots*, co-wrote the book. Millions who had seen the television series based on *Roots* now read *The Autobiography of Malcolm X*, regardless of their race or politics. Also in the news and on the nation's mind was the Black Panther Party for Self Defense. Long-serving FBI Director J. Edgar Hoover considered it his personal mission (some said "vendetta") to monitor activities of the Black Panthers for any sign of revolutionary leanings.

Perplexed as to how Malcolm X had escaped my awareness during my high school years, I now studied his work and combed every page of his autobiography. How had his very public presence eluded me until *four years after his death?* As a college freshman, I now found myself intrigued by this charismatic man. It pained me to read his words, which contrasted with my ignorance of the plight of African-Americans since colonial days. As I read the truth behind the black experience in America, my lack of awareness of that history stung with embarrassment.

One day during February of that freshman year, I was walking to the cafeteria at FPCC when a black militant group I had not previously heard of first caught my attention by recruiting members on campus. A loud public address system they had cranked way up played a recorded speech by the Black Panther Party leader, Eldridge Cleaver. The album was entitled *DIG!*—a then-contemporary term meaning "Check this out!" Cleaver, the Black Panther Party's Minister of

Information, made some very inflammatory comments about injustice in America. He spared no language in his remarks.

The next day, a group of white students from the very conservative Young Americans for Freedom (YAF), complained to the college president. The president decided to come down to the cafeteria and pull the record off the turntable. He did so, and scratched it badly in the process. He told the student newspaper that his intent was to "confiscate" the record. Things did not go just as he planned. Five black militants stood up, neither amused nor intimidated. They lunged at the college president to "re-confiscate" the album. A brawl broke out, and campus police were called in. Several militants were arrested after order was restored. I heard those guys were charged with battery and had to post bail.

Later in the spring of 1970, a group of militants planned to honor the life of Malcolm X on the anniversary of his death by lowering the American flag to half-mast on the student commons. The conservative white group (YAF) objected to lowering the flag since Malcolm X was a figure they saw as "revolutionary," and took it upon themselves to raise it back to full staff. Another melee broke out on the quadrangle. In the subsequent struggle, the American flag was ripped and dragged on the ground. The black militants were arrested. The white group from YAF was not. Decrying what they saw as a racist response by the college, the militant group immediately organized a boycott of classes and called for a moratorium in the spring of 1970.

The boycott and moratorium were focused on specific injustices. Issues included freedom of speech, a demand that Black Studies classes be added to the curriculum, and an explanation as to why a disproportionate number of blacks to whites were serving on the front lines in the Vietnam War. When the school resisted the boycott, clandestine acts of reprisal broke out. Unknown individuals sprayed mace into the doorways of classrooms. That proved a remarkably effective way to dismiss a few classes in a hurry! A couple of fires "mysteriously" broke out on campus. Finally, a moratorium was called.

Authorities on campus called in a group of FBI agents and Saint Louis Police Intelligence units. Some black students questioned whether Federal Bureau of Investigation officers were sent to investigate or perhaps to intimidate free expression on campus. Local police intelligence units were likewise chided for arriving long after any intelligent person already knew what the issues were. The common tools of police work, guns, tear gas and clubs, seemed much more in evidence than pens and yellow pads. Dossiers and COINTELPRO (counterintelligence program) intelligence-gathering by the FBI and the local police, began in earnest.

Order was eventually restored to the community college campus and surrounding neighborhoods. Black Studies classes were instituted in the curriculum of Saint Louis' three junior college campuses: Forest Park, Meramec, and Florissant Valley. "Rap Sessions" were also held by militant groups along with sympathetic faculty and other faculty members whose main desire was a return to normalcy on the campuses. These sessions were organized for the airing of grievances and discussion of issues unrelated to any class work. They took place in student lounges most every day. Interested people who wanted to attend the sessions got together by passing along information via word of mouth. Posters also announced plans for "Rap Sessions" at a certain time in the student lounge. More informal discussions took place when someone who wanted to chat with another person about a political issue would say, "let me rap to you for a few minutes." These sessions had nothing to do with Hip-Hop, which did not come along for another ten years.

Many black students who didn't care about revolutionary

or militant agendas joined fraternities or sororities. These students usually came from affluent families or from families trained for generations to be submissive and pleasant, no matter what the personal cost. They called themselves "Black Greeks," a term which infuriated the militant students. It was clear that mainstream fraternities and sororities would continue their policy of ignoring current events on campus, in the Saint Louis metro area, or on the national level. We were indoctrinated to think that Black Greeks strove to emulate white fraternities and sororities, but with a soulful twist to make them palatable. Plus, Brothers and Sisters were often encouraged by parents who had sent their young people to college so they might blend in with the established social and political order. That mindset was totally at odds with the revolutionary and social organizations on campus, and a bitter distancing of these groups simmered like a not-so-dormant volcano. On each of the Saint Louis campuses, rivalries erupted into open disrespect and occasional acts of vandalism. The issue: who would recruit more black students. The frats and sororities dominated the party scene and loved playing card games like Bid Whist in the lounges between classes—and even in lieu of going to class. The militants responded with ridicule.

How was an intelligent black student who simply wanted to get a good education so he could become the next James Bond supposed to react to these opposing forces all around him? For the most part, I was an unattached observer throughout most of these struggles during my freshman year and the summer following. I was re-learning my past nineteen years on the planet. Militants taunted "serious students" who deferred participation in activism:

> *"I'll help you all get free, as soon as I get my Master's Degree."*

"I would help in the fight, but gotta keep my grades uptight!"

CHAPTER SEVENTEEN

Vietnam and the Beginning of Activism

MY LOYALTIES WERE TORN between the two worlds, which never seemed to meet on any common ground. It was all black and white—in a philosophical sense, as well as a racial one. Should I join the goodie-goodie blacks who were sent to school to become good citizens and members of the middle class—at the expense of their heritage—and often their identity? Would I be true to my own people, whose historical struggle during the days of African slave trade, slavery in the New World, and then emancipation which often meant slavery to a paycheck or to a plantation boss? Why was there no choice that would allow me to respect the best of both traditions?

In the end, I suppose my experience up to that point ordained my choice. I shared very little common experience with the "Black Greeks" whose parents were well-enough off to hope that their offspring might take another modest step up the socio-economic ladder and be grateful for that chance. My own father had been an elevator "boy," and had lost faith in the system when he was told he was no longer needed there. My mother worked fifty or sixty hours a week in the dire hope that her sons would not end up disillusioned like so many other African-Americans in The Ville of North St. Louis. "Greekdom," whether on campus in polite parties or later in life, in some polite but powerless job was not on my radar screen.

Once my eyes had been opened to the truth of my ancestors' abuse for generation after generation, I could not be silent. Eventually, I joined the campus militant group as an inquisitive person seeking knowledge. My roles for expression became poet, actor, and political satirist. I came to see myself as the city version of a country bumpkin. I could identify with the traditional tales of Ole Jack, setting out to seek his fortune in an unknown world beyond his Mamma's parlor. My Mamma's tattered doilies tried their hardest to cover the frayed arms of a worn sofa and a rocking chair whose squeak was not so much a lullaby as a cry for maintenance. Like Jack of old, I had very little idea of what a black militant was and even less idea of what a fraternity or sorority was. I sensed that artistic expression would be my future. So, in compensation for my delayed entrance into political awareness, I sought roles, platforms and stages with the African-American artistic community. Organizations such as the Black Artists Group (BAG) and several receptive ministers of civil rights churches invited me to recite the poetry of Langston Hughes and The Last Poets. Occasionally, I was invited to take major roles performing in local concerts.

The stage seemed natural to me. I felt the stage was where my energies were most needed. In my gut, I could feel a hunger to succeed as a performer. I would spend days memorizing long passages from black literature and perform them at Rap sessions. These performances were often staged between compelling and sometimes horrific reminiscences of men who had recently returned from the Vietnam War. The stories from Southeast Asia—of men spraying Agent Orange defoliant on plants, and napalm (often called "liquid saran wrap") on people—were common. Some vets talked of a "game" some soldiers had called Rollie Pollie. The heads of Viet Cong dead were cut off and rolled down a hill. The person whose particular head reached the bottom of the hill first won the game. Occasionally, I was slotted just after one of the heroes who had marched with Dr. King or protested with H. Rap Brown, such as Stokley Carmichael, Huey P. Newton, Eldridge Cleaver, or Bobby Seale. These human rights, civil rights, and black power icons were all national and international figures. They shaped my world view and gave me a new perspective on issues that were previously "hidden in plain view."

Studying these same people in the classes of professors in History, Political Science, Sociology, English Literature, and Black Studies was the essential key to the knowledge I needed to grow intellectually and spiritually.

No book or individual had more impact on my psyche than Malcolm X and his autobiography, co-authored by Alex Haley, author of the historical bestseller, *Roots*. To me, the brilliance and courage of Malcolm X have never been equaled by any other political figure.

My education and passage into maturity was launched full steam ahead by my first trip to Chicago!

CHAPTER EIGHTEEN

The Windy City

I WAS A SOPHOMORE in junior college when I first traveled to Chicago. A group called Project Ahead funded the trip for underserved minority students who qualified academically. My participation was the work of Tanzi Mayer and Rick Reynolds, both former counselors at Sumner High, and two of my early mentors. After leaving SHS, they joined the community college staff and headed the organization Project Ahead.

Seeing downtown Chicago for the first time was a magical moment in my life. When our van turned off Interstate 55 and made the curve that brought us down to Lakeshore Drive just a block from Lake Michigan, my eyes widened in wonder. To our left rose the incredible architecture of the Chicago Loop. To our right was the vast expanse of Lake Michigan—no opposite shore in sight.

The next morning, I stood in my room on the eleventh floor of the Days Inn on Lake Shore Drive at Ontario, and took in what looked to me like an ocean view. A mid-continent kid, I had never seen the ocean either. It was 1970, two years after the Chicago Seven had made history disrupting the Democratic National Convention just a few blocks from where I now stood. What mark might I leave on history—a junior college kid who didn't seem to be making any progress toward his goal of becoming the first black James Bond? Would I make any mark at all? I wondered what the future had in store for me.

Our sponsors saw that we toured all the highlights of Chicago. We saw the Cabrini-Green housing projects—setting for the TV show *Good Times*—the Magnificent Mile, which included the Shedd Aquarium, the Chicago Museum of Art, the DuSable Museum of African American History, Buckingham Fountain, the Wrigley Building, the *Chicago Tribune*, Water Tower Place, the Sears Tower and the John Hancock Building. At the foot of the Tribune Tower, I noticed irregularities in the stone wall just above my head. On closer inspection, I realized that what appeared to be building defects were actually stones from ancient structures, identified by small brass plaques. There was a rough stone from the wall of Baghdad, a bit of Jerusalem's Wailing Wall, a small piece of masonry from the Houses of Parliament in London. Another square-like piece came from the Great Pyramid at Giza. History was all around me!

The John Hancock Building was another powerful experience. Twice as tall as the Gateway Arch in Saint Louis, the black edifice tapered almost out of sight. Once inside, we entered elevators that sucked us up into the clouds in a matter of seconds. Looking down on the city and the lake from the observation deck, I saw the grid of orderly Chicago streets. The panorama was like a view from an airplane, yet I was standing in a building. It was a lot to take in.

We took the Grey Line Deluxe Bus Tour, visited museum after museum, and ate like wild animals! The food of Chicago was endless—and all good! I discovered Indian food that night in Chicago, selected from an awe-inspiring array of ethnic offerings. Back home in Saint Louis, Italian and Mexican restaurants seemed exotic, but here in "the Windy City," every breeze seemed to present the aroma of a new ethnic concoction. Chicago had opened my eyes to great architecture, to an ocean-sized lake, to historical and art museums, and now it was opening my nostrils to cuisines from around the world.

The following night, we walked down Michigan Avenue to the Schubert Theatre, where we sat in awe as the musical *HAIR* came alive on the stage. It was the great musical's first run. While I was not sure if a fabulously-staged musical was part of my Future James Bond training, I knew that I had truly entered the Age of Aquarius!

That night in the dark theatre, with new musical styles driven into my brain, I felt truly on the edge of an unknown world, certainly not the world as I knew it so far. Looking back on that visit, it seemed that Chicago had some of the best elements of New York City and Los Angeles combined. Walking down Michigan Avenue has the feel of Broadway in Lower Manhattan. Watching skateboarders and sunbathers along Lakeshore Drive in the summertime has a genuine LA feel.

CHAPTER NINETEEN

Awakening the Sleeping Giant

I MET CINDIE, who became my first wife, when we were both students at UMSL. We belonged to the Association of Black Collegians (ABC). When I transferred from Forest Park Community College, I helped to found the UMSL chapter and became its first board chair in 1971.

We were smitten with each other and dated often. As love and nature would have it, she was soon carrying our baby boy, Damon Emmanuel. We married while college students, suddenly realizing the difficulty to balance two academic schedules, the demands of a newborn, and two work-study jobs. There was no budget for dates, dinners at home were meager, and nights were short. For the first time in my young life, I truly empathized with my parents' struggle to keep utility bills paid and food on the table.

In early 1972 while passing through the student union one day, I was stopped by an instructor who asked me to apply for the Metropolitan Leadership Program Fellowship funded through the Danforth Foundation. I was game, especially since my only income was coming from a work-study job at a restaurant on Oakland Avenue near campus. Stan and Biggies was owned by St. Louis Cardinal legend, Stan "The Man" Musial.

I applied for one of the thirteen Danforth Fellowships. All total, 300 people applied for the thirteen spots. The competition was held at St. Louis University and lasted four days. We participants went from room to room, sitting in interviews with college instructors, professors, and Danforth Foundation officials. Each of the thirteen fellowships meant a $10,000 stipend for each for two years while attending any college or university in the St. Louis area. I applied for the 1973 and 1974 school years. The program included two summer internships in an agency that was related to our major areas of study. Many companies signed up to accept the young interns who won the fellowships. I had decided to major in journalism. At first, my sights were set on the University of Missouri-Columbia Journalism School. When I realized the fellowship had to be local, I revised my plan, thinking that I would seek a dual major in U.S. History and Journalism at the University Missouri-St. Louis.

At one point, a panel asked a group of us to draw a crayon picture showing where we envisioned ourselves in ten years. Being a devoted follower of the reporting of Walter Cronkite and Dan Rather on CBS, I longed to be a journalist with that network. For some reason, however, I drew a picture of me on stage in front of an audience of several hundred people. My "goal picture" showed me holding a microphone.

I had recently joined a poet group called the Messengers. It consisted of four students from Forest Park Community College who recited fiery political poetry in front of audiences in student lounges and at political rallies. My material was from the albums of The Last Poets, a fantastic group from Harlem, New York, who performed with *djembe* drums, *shekere, conga* and *jun-jun.*

The Messengers made no money. It wasn't a job, but a mission for me to impart knowledge through the spoken word. My son Damon was born on Sept. 11, 1972. Damon's mother and I desperately needed income for life's basics—food, shelter, heat, and clothing. Cindie and I had married in love, but reality was tearing us apart. I remember, on the afternoon of the fourth day of the Danforth competition, I had only a quarter in my pocket. The officials said they would contact all of us by special delivery registered mail on that Friday afternoon. I walked through Fairgrounds Park, near our apartment on Grand and Natural Bridge Avenue, meditating and praying for positive results as I held that quarter in my hands.

On a Friday afternoon, arriving home from my last class at 4 p.m., I slumped onto the sofa. Moments later, I heard a knock on the door. The mailman instructed me to sign for a registered letter. As he walked away, I sat on the front steps of my apartment. It was May 1973. I looked up at the cloudy sky and went into my meditation "zone" holding that letter, trying to divine its contents. A calm peacefulness overtook me. Slowly opening the envelope, I unfolded the letter and looked up at the sky once again. I sighed, focused on the letterhead, and began reading:

> Dear Mr. Norfolk,
>   Congratulations. You have been chosen as a recipient of the 1973-1974 Metropolitan Leadership Program grant from the Danforth Foundation.

My internships followed my journalism study. *Proud Magazine*, owned by Ernie McMillian of the St. Louis (football) Cardinals, was my first assignment. Additional internships with the *St. Louis Sentinel* newspaper, owned by Howard B. Woods, and the *St. Louis American*, owned by Dr. Donald Suggs, would complete my training. A ray of afternoon sunshine burst through the clouds.

In 1972, I was upgraded. Having received a grant from the Danforth Foundation and the Metropolitan Leadership Program to attend the University of Missouri-Saint Louis (UMSL), I found myself with academic work at a new level. Attending what some called the "mini-Harvard of the Midwest" was a shock in nearly every way. Thankful for my TM training, I met the challenges of academic and social adjustment excitedly. Campus life was much more intense, both in terms of academics and extracurricular activities. UMSL professors took no prisoners. They expected focus and critical thinking of a level that was entirely new to me. One day, sitting in the third row of European History, I realized I was thinking *Sean Connery must have taken this course to acquire his grasp of Cold War intrigue.*

It didn't take me long to adjust to the rigors of this commuter campus. Fortunately, my teachers at Charles Sumner High had drilled excellent study habits into my juvenile skull. Without them, I might have succeeded in community college, but not at UMSL.

After class, I was beginning to feel a sense of self-confidence that would manifest itself in invitations to campus leadership roles. Within a year, I became chair of the Black Student Union, which in that day was almost like being student body president for the black students on campus. Leadership, I quickly learned, can be exhilarating one moment and humbling within the flash of an eye.

That spring, a flyer circulated around the campuses in Saint Louis. It announced a national forum and rally to be hosted by the Black Panther Party for Self Defense to take place at Temple University in Philadelphia, Pennsylvania, in just a few months. Surely, I thought, a prominent student leader from "the mini-Harvard of the Midwest" should be on hand to experience such a momentous event.

At that time, the Philadelphia chief of police was Frank Rizzo, a cop whose reputation for the confrontational suppression of anti-Vietnam War marches and black militant organizations was legendary. At UMSL and campuses across the country, sign-up sheets for students to carpool to Philly appeared on message boards in student unions.

I signed up for the adventure of going to a major revolutionary event as a once-in-a-lifetime opportunity to observe history in the making. My carpool list included two women I knew and three men, unknown to me. In the car on the long drive from St. Louis to Philadelphia, we listened to the radio and talked politics. We debated issues such as birth control as a form of genocide, and the ethnic imbalance of American foot soldiers in Vietnam. We ate catch-all meals assembled from our rucksacks and a few grocery store stops. We slept sprawled across each other while the designated driver pressed on.

The anticipation of what we were about to experience was palpable.

When we arrived in the "City of Brotherly Love," the love seemed to be missing. We felt the serious tension in the city, indeed in the entire state of Pennsylvania. J. Edgar Hoover's FBI was on full alert, as were the state and local police forces, and the Pennsylvania National Guard. Several altercations had broken out between the flood of college students arriving from campuses nationwide and the uniformed, shield and billy club-bearing forces of Police Chief Frank Rizzo. J. Edgar Hoover's cadres were busy in unmarked surveillance vans and as plainclothes men on the streets, filling out dossiers on any group connected to civil rights, human rights, and anti-war protesting. Hoover launched COINTELPRO during those times. The intent was to stop demonstrations not only by those advocating governmental overthrow, but in many cases, it targeted those who simply advocated societal change. On the streets of Philadelphia that week, it became apparent that, to Hoover, the ends justified the means.

I found myself feeling one part country bumpkin and one part fledgling James Bond wannabe, walking into an atmosphere as highly charged as a military battle zone. Shootouts between various police elements and cadres of the Black Panther Party provided national TV news all that year. White hippies intent on ending the war in

Vietnam demonstrated under the banner of Students for a Democratic Society (SDS). Their more radical brethren, the Weathermen or Weather-Underground, were present but less distinguishable. The Weathermen saw their mission as creating mayhem in order to bring the Establishment to its knees. What was the Establishment? It was the government with all of its control mechanisms: the military, CIA, FBI, and Secret Service. Add to that the cigar smoke-filled boardrooms of the largest corporations, those who feasted on war profits and bought congressmen to stave off any legislation aimed at better working conditions, higher wages, and worker rights.

The Selective Service System was re-instituted. A national military draft was revived during the Vietnam War. Hundreds of thousands of young men were snatched from colleges and civilian jobs. They were sent to Southeast Asia to fight a war whose ultimate goal Congress never defined. Fifty-eight thousand three hundred and three of them died. Many thought the war was not justifiable. The Johnson and Nixon administrations were accused of committing war crimes— not just by young blacks, but by white male Catholic priests and nuns as well. College students began burning their draft cards in public protest. If you were drafted, you could go to war, apply as a "conscientious objector," claim a religious exemption like Muhammad Ali and be charged with a crime, or escape into Canada. Young, white, left-wing, radical college students were also making this pilgrimage to Philadelphia.

When my friends and I arrived in the area of South Philly where we were to be housed, we drove through extremely narrow streets of old row houses, so unlike the broad streets and detached homes of St. Louis. We lugged our duffels upstairs, into an apartment where twelve of us men were to stay. The women who had accompanied us cross-country were housed in separate quarters in another apartment.

When my three new friends and I settled into our male-only apartment, a group of older men began pulling out weapons. Having never been in close proximity to military-style rifles and handguns before, I realized I was rooming with true militants. I watched in awe as men began to assemble them, attaching screw-on barrels to what looked like army-issue weapons. This arsenal was pulled from duffel bags that looked like the ones in which we'd brought our changes of clothes from college. Each man was ordered to stand guard on shifts day and night. I was ordered by the group leader to stand guard from 3 a.m. to 5 a.m. at the back window. When I protested, "I just came to experience the conference," the gruff reply was to stand watch as ordered. It was not an option or a request. At 3 a.m. I was awakened, given a tutorial on loading and unloading a carbine, and the weapon was shoved into my hands. Directed to a dinette chair placed in front of a window overlooking the back alley, I was told to sit, stay alert, and watch for suspicious activity. Silently, the dawn pushed back the night as I saw my life flashing before my eyes and remembered the order to yell "Ambush!" to wake everyone up if "the Philadelphia pigs come!" Well, no "pigs" came, and at 5:30 a.m. everyone ate breakfast and we went to Temple University for the morning opening of the conference and rally. I made sure to take my belongings with me, as I had no intention of returning to that row house. That evening, I booked myself into a Holiday Inn. The country bumpkin was learning to choose his friends.

The first keynote speaker was Michael Tabor of the Black Panther Party's Philadelphia chapter. He gave an electrifying and impassioned speech on the state of human rights and injustices in America. After Tabor had concluded, I sat alone, surrounded by groups who had driven in from other states. We gathered at the field house at Temple University. It was full of people waiting for the next speaker to take the stage. To my left, a group of eight or nine white "free love" hippies started kissing and necking amongst themselves. This took place in front of the very group of older men I had encountered at the row house. The militant group leader jumped up, yelling and swearing at the hippies to get away from the area with all that "weird crap!" Suddenly from nowhere, a swarm of Black Panther security forces wearing black berets, black maxi-coats, black paratrooper boots, and dark sunglasses came running up the aisles.

When the Black Panther patrol arrived at the scene of the disturbance, their leader demanded to know what the problem was. When the row house guy said he was upset about those damn hippies, he was told by the Black Panther leader to shut up, sit down, or move to another area of the arena.

"We aren't having any of this reactionary crap in here," the Panther leader shouted. The rowdy group grumbled and settled back down. The terrified hippies regrouped but refrained from any further display of "free love" that morning. The Black Panther guards stationed themselves strategically around the area to make sure everyone behaved themselves. It was amazing to watch this interchange of culture, political fervor, power, and history unfold.

Speaking of history, before I left Philadelphia I made sure to visit the First Continental Congress building (Liberty Hall) and the Liberty Bell. After all, I had to experience both ends of the political spectrum.

For four years beginning in the fall of 1970, I attended the University of Missouri at Saint Louis under the Danforth Foundation Fellowship. Having had spent the previous year struggling socially at Forest Park Community College, I was primed for a step up both academically and socially. Little did I know during my first few hours on the UMSL campus that the years ahead would be an eye-opening time for me.

My studies were challenging, but my extracurricular experiences were even more so. Those years were my introduction to social action, to political militancy. New ideas were thrown at me daily, and my rest was often interrupted by sudden dream-state realizations. The university years ought to be a mind-expanding time for young people, and my UMSL years were certainly that for me.

Notwithstanding the growth experiences I had benefited from in high school, my UMSL years introduced me to historical figures in the civil rights movement and their forebears. I read the speeches and essays of W.E.B. Dubois, immersed myself in "Afro/American" poetry (much deeper than in high school), and began to form a personal, social, and political philosophy. It seemed like playing with Tinker Toys: take an idea from here, an idea from there, and tinker to see if they fit with the help of a conjunctive concept from somewhere else entirely. Professors helped. Friends helped. But it was work that, ultimately, I had to do for myself.

The university years added a philosophical layer to my personality as a performer. This liberating poetry had been my foundation as a performer. Of course, it was laden with dark experiences of African-Americans, and it added to those wonderful rhythms of the music of the time. Now I added the work of progressive thinkers—and my own troubled thinking—plus the insights of mentors both on campus and off.

Comedy would come next. I became a stand-up comedian in 1975, near the end of my time at UMSL. With contemporary poetry, political satire, the rhythmic heart of a performer, and my newly-acquired political consciousness, I was ready to find situations, issues, and causes with which to energize my whole act. Dick Gregory and Richard Pryor would be people I emulated for my professional growth. It would be a rocky road.

CHAPTER TWENTY

Moving the Cat

WHEN I WAS IN COLLEGE AT **UMSL**, my parents moved to another apartment and they were able to transport everything in their possession, except the cat, which refused to leave the place where he had grown from a kitten. I was given the dubious duty of going to get this feline and bringing it over to the new apartment in my car. How difficult could it be? It was very, very difficult, as a matter of fact. This guy was not declawed and was around two years old, a tomcat, that I had never met before. He had no idea who I was.

The apartment was empty. I went upstairs to the second floor where he was and spoke to him in my calmest voice. In return, he hissed and wailed the frightful cry of a cat in great distress. Every time I tried to pick him up, he ran frantically from corner to corner, down the hall, from room to room. Once, when I thought I had him cornered, he climbed the wall with his claws and leaped over my head, running into yet another room. I decided to close the doors of the room, eliminating his exits. I went back to my car. Since it was wintertime, I put on my leather gloves, determined this cat and I were about to have a showdown. Gathering my thoughts, I planned the exit route. I left my car door open as well as the front door. Upon arriving back where he was and summoning my inner ninja, I calmly approached to subdue him. Failing in subtlety, I lunged for him, a move he didn't like at all. Scratching my wrists with all four paws, he bit me through the gloves, wailed, peed on me, and writhed in his quest to break free.

Cats, when terrified, will claw, bite and scratch at everything within reach. This guy grabbed ahold of the right sleeve of my winter coat and wouldn't let go! I pried one set of claws loose and he made contact with the other three! At one point, he broke loose and used me like a tree, running up my chest and over my back. I deftly whirled about and caught him again by his belly and back without getting my face scratched. I managed to get the tuft of hair and skin behind his neck and carried him the way mother cats carry their kittens. He angrily swished at the air with his "terrible claws and gnashing teeth!" I ran down the stairs and flung him into the back seat and slammed the door.

Puffing and panting, I pulled off the leather gloves, which had saved me from severe pain and loss of blood. Driving to the new address was no problem. After parking, I realized that now I would have to get him out of my car. The wily fellow had disappeared under the car seat, and he refused to come out. *Alrighty then,* I thought, *this is going to be as difficult as getting him out of the old house.* I opened both doors on the passenger side and, making sure he didn't take off running, put my trusty gloves back on. His green and yellow eyes stared back at me from his lair under the car seat. His woeful moaning resumed. Several of our new neighbors stood outside talking to each other on their front porch. I thought, *Boy, are they going to see a spectacle!* The tomcat and I didn't disappoint them.

Determined that getting him out of the car was going to take as much effort as extracting him from the old apartment—especially with spectators agog—I sized up the situation. I walked around the car and opened the two doors on the driver's side. The cat turned under the bench seat and checked me out. I casually crept back around to the passenger side. Seeing his tail swishing back and forth, I grabbed it and yanked! He wailed and buried his front claws into the carpeting under the seat. When I saw his hind legs, I grabbed them and pulled! He wailed even louder, clawing and ripping at the carpeting. I pulled him out of the car, immediately grabbed his scruffy little neck, and carried the beast into the new apartment. His four claws were flailing at the air and the new neighbors were all looking in amazement, wondering ... *What in the world?*

Opening the door to the apartment, I flung Thomas onto an overstuffed chair and slammed the front door. Thomas settled into his new digs with a lot of extra care from Mom and Dad. The neighbors always seemed to be afraid of him for some reason when he ventured outside.

CHAPTER TWENTY-ONE

Moonlighting as the Real Me

As A KID, I grew up on the humor of Red Skelton, Lucille Ball, Phyllis Diller, the Three Stooges, Laurel & Hardy, Abbott & Costello, Sid Caesar and Imogene Coca, and Dick Van Dyke. In 1975, I began hearing of a standup comedian who my friends claimed was incredibly talented. Richard Pryor was a masterful standup comedian of monologs and physical comedy. His material was caustic, politically-charged, and really funny. Pryor made no apology for his African-American dialect or uppity tone. Serious about developing my own comedy career, I studied every aspect of his routines carefully. Pryor's full-body physicality, sharp-witted repartee, and sassy heckler come-backs impressed me immensely, as did his catalog of exaggerated facial expressions. I was an instant Richard Pryor disciple. His comedic genius was undeniable. Despite his occasional risqué language, Pryor remains unmatched by anyone else on the scene even to this day.

I also studied Dick Gregory for the political satire he brought to the stage. Gregory's presentation was more sophisticated than Pryor's, and his content was radical. Gregory molded my perspective of this society and the world through his witty and insightful monologs. His clever routines took real life circumstances and molded them into political satire at its finest level. I learned that it was possible to be funny while making a pointed social comment. Gregory's commitment to the civil rights movement of the 1960s was the foundation of his professional work. I watched as he sprinkled the beginning of an innocuous, seemingly G-rated night club set with humor any parent might identify with. After warming audiences up, Gregory unleashed stinging blows about racism, warmongering, economic inequality and other social and political failures. He fired up early 1970s audiences, for example, talking about those who worried aloud about demonstrators shouting and carrying protest signs and disdaining immigrants coming across America's borders. To me, it was inspiring.

For those people who were satisfied with prevailing political conditions, Gregory's punchline silenced the house: "If anybody has the right to say 'America, love it or leave it,' that would be the American Indians. When they say it, that means the big trip across The Pond, baby! If you don't realize how this land was forcibly taken from Native People, you don't know your history!"

Next, I studied George Carlin for his mastery of word-play. Carlin gave his audiences so much fun with words by his outlandish puns, silly poems and bashed taboos; he was amazing! Like Gregory's,

Carlin's material was sharp and politically charged, but Carlin was a real wordsmith, and his audiences often forgave his most divisive political comments out of sheer delight in his wit and wordplay.

Don Rickles was unrelenting in his face-to-face put-downs of audience members, whether they were heckling or not. I could adopt some of his rapid fire diatribes when I had to put a heckler "back in his place." In the rougher night clubs in East St. Louis and The Ville, I opened with a barrage of Rickles-like put-downs. They worked like a charm. Anyone who experienced Rickles' caustic humor must surely remember it forever.

The fatherly comedy of Bill Cosby, who followed Gregory into stardom, impressed me for his perfect timing and facial expressions. When he raised his eyebrows and pursed his lips, whether onstage or in an episode of *The Cosby Show*, a TV staple of the 1980s, every viewer took a deep breath and awaited the punch line. His routines brought the house down every time. I saw the potential of taking the business of standup comedy and thought "I have found my niche."

One time I treated myself on a birthday to a ticket to see him at the Fox Theatre in St. Louis. I was more than impressed. I was sitting in the mezzanine watching him as he came out and sat in a Lazy Boy chair onstage. A woman rushed in a few minutes late and sat in the second row with two young blond children. The Cos stopped his routine and starred at them positioning themselves in their chairs. He cleared his throat and asked; "was there heavy traffic, Ma'am?"

Immediately her son yelled out, "My Dad was barbecuing a goat, and we were watching!" A fifteen-minute killer routine ensued that brought the house down!

Richard Pryor's incredibly raw comedy, Gregory's political satire, Cosby's pantomime, Carlin's wordplay, the Three Stooges' slapstick, and Don Rickles' take-no-prisoners attitude were the perfect models for me to emulate. I purchased the LPs of the party albums of Rudy Ray Moore. I learned by memory "Stagger Lee," "Shine," "Pimping Sam" and "The Signifying Monkey." I would intersperse the raw material with a powerful spoken word group out of New York's Harlem called The Last Poets. Some stand-out pieces, "True Blues," "E-Pluribus Unum," "The Mean Machine," and "The Whiteman's Got a God Complex," all struck me as potential cornerstones for my repertoire. Pieces were written and performed by Umar Bin Hasson, Suliaman El Hadi, and Jala Mansur Nuriddin aka Alafia Pudim, all original members of the Last Poets. They all took on African names to identify with their communities, their "roots" prior to the slave trade. They arrived on the scene as the Black Nationalist, or Black Power movement took hold in America when Dr. King was assassinated in 1968.

One evening all alone, I ventured out to a local jazz club called Mr. Connors Jazz House on Natural Bridge Road and asked the night club owners if I could perform during the fifteen-minute band breaks. They all agreed and said, "If you clear it with the jazz trio's leader, David Hines, you can go on."

David gladly agreed, saying, "We would like to be entertained for a change instead of being the show." I have always felt that my career really began at that time, in May of 1975.

My next gig was a regular spot at Lou & Lawrence's Gold Palace, the last night club in the once vibrant Gas Light Square area in Midtown St. Louis. Comedian Rodney Winfield had cut his teeth there earlier before he went on a world tour with The Supremes. When we later worked together on a St. Louis radio show hosted by Hank Thompson, Rodney quipped: "Performing with Bobby is like working with Hamlet!"

Eventually, I found confidence enough to introduce my

original material, using the "Pryor model." When done correctly, the African-American audiences in the local night clubs really liked the risqué humor. When I performed for well-educated upper middle class black-and-white crowds, the political satire was preferred with a sprinkle of blue humor.

At the Funny Bone Comedy Clubs, they loved the edgy humor, too, and they dug the way I delivered it! "Age of the Whiskey" was a favorite:

"A guy walked into a bar and said, "I'd like a glass of six-year-old whiskey, please!" The bartender, not wanting to be bothered by this chump who probably wouldn't know the difference, brought him a glass of bar whiskey.

The customer sniffed, tasted, and said "This is some cheap bar whiskey, sir. I asked for six-year-old whiskey." The bartender thought *I knew that was some crappy whiskey, but I'll pour him some two-year-old whiskey because the six-year bottles are down in the cellar, and I don't want to go down there right now.*

The customer tasted and exclaimed, "This is two years old, sir. Are we not communicating? I asked for six-year-old scotch!"

In surprise the bartender said, "I'm so sorry, sir; my mistake." The bartender thought, *I'm going to test this guy and see if he is on the level.* He poured the customer a drink from an eight-year bottle.

The customer turned the glass up and shouted that was a fantastic drink—even two years earlier than I asked. "May I have the six-year whiskey now?"

The bartender broke down and said, "Sir, all your drinks are on the house. I'll need to go down to the cellar to get your bottle."

A drunk had been watching the exchange from the corner of the bar. He staggered over to the customer, saying, "Hey, I saw what you were doing over here. That's some pretty impressive tasting. Then handing the customer a shot glass, he said, "Here, taste this."

The customer took the glass and turned it up, taking it all into his mouth. As he swished the drink around his mouth, he suddenly spat it all out, gagging. When he regained his composure, the customer said, "Hey! That wasn't whiskey; that was pee!"

The drunk said, "I know that fool; I want you to tell me *how old it is!*"

Another crowd favorite went like this:

One day two women were standing in front of their houses arguing about which was the worst pain a woman could suffer, menstrual cramps or childbirth. In the midst of this heated discussion, a male postal worker walked up delivering mail. Seeing him, one woman said, "Sir, would you help us solve this disagreement? Which is the worst pain—menstrual cramps or child birth?"

The postman paused, became thoughtful and said, "I'm not sure ladies, but have you ever been kicked in the balls before? Now *that's* pain!"

There is much more blue humor I used in those days, but it's not fit for this book. Sorry!

The blue material was used as a setup to later deliver political satire. To me, there was always a method to the madness. The work of a satirist/activist on a creative level was a kind of high-wire act. As Lincoln Perry (Stepin Fetchit) famously told the National Negro Baseball legend, Leroy Satchel Paige, "Disarm with humor those who *think* they hate you. Then dazzle them with your talents!"

Zack, Mack and I eventually got to open shows for Ahmed Jamal and Gil Scott Heron. By that time, I realized that I was able to find the bridge to become a "cross-over comedian," one who could play both black crowds and white crowds, Hispanics, and blended crowds—all with equal success. We opened for the hottest music acts in America when they came to perform in St. Louis, but did not go out on the road with them. We performed at places like Kiel Auditorium, the Chase Park Plaza, the steamboat *Admiral*, and several venues in East St. Louis, Illinois. It was gratifying to hear other professionals tell me that I was doing "killer shows" every weekend.

The irony here is the fact that, while my counterculture performance career was flowering, I had a full-time job as a National Park Service (NPS) Ranger at the Gateway Arch in St. Louis. An article from *The Riverfront Times*, a weekly paper of that period, featured my dual careers in 1978. The article was very powerful. It laid out my daytime work for "the Establishment" alongside my radical nighttime gigs. The same week I was written up by United Press International, the Associated Press and made three local TV newscasts! In 1978, I felt ready to soar to the top. Engagements with magicians Karl Grice and Harold D. Russell added a special touch to the music and comedy. Having started standup three years earlier, I now felt approval from local colleagues as well as visiting national stars.

After two years of solo shows, I felt the need for an emcee to introduce me when I came on stage. My good friend Johnnie McHaynes proved to be the man. We had met while attending Forest Park Community College, where we were in the same political circles. Johnnie had fantastic quick wit and was a master at *Jonening*, a style of routine in which two performers just light into one another with words, not fists.

Some very creative African-American comedy has spawned from disparaging other folks' mamas and daddies! Culturally, this verbal sword fight consisted of two guys making jokes and improvising pieces about the others' relatives. Mothers, fathers, sisters, brothers, aunts, uncles, granddads and grandmas—even cousins were not immune to playful abuse. Playing *The Dozens*, talking about people's relatives—a synonym for Jonening—was Mack's specialty. Mack remained the evil genius of heckler comebacks. White audiences love this witty repartee also, but it resonated best with predominantly African-American groups like those at Maurice's Gold Coast Lounge on Olive Boulevard. Maurice had a "Back Room" where all comics—black and white—would try out new material. We alternated with The Funny Bone Comedy Club to see how material played to a predominantly white crowd. He consented to be my emcee, but Mack was frightened to go on stage alone. He asked a mutual friend of ours, Zachary Scott Carey, to be his partner on the stage. Big Zack was thrilled to do it. Oh, by the way, Mack was about five foot eleven inches tall and weighed close to 300 pounds. Zack was about six foot eight inches tall and weighed 350 to 400 pounds. They were big boys, as a matter of fact, and that's how they billed themselves: "The Biggest Act in Show Business." They peppered their routines with hilarious "fat jokes."

I sat with Mack one day to think of a unique way for them to introduce me. We brainstormed and somehow came up with this: The rhythm and blues (R&B) group, The Spinners, had a popular song out in 1976 called "The Rubberband Man." I would put on fifteen coats and jackets to look as big as Zack & Mack. After I got the sixth coat on, Big Zack would put the others on by pulling both lapels of each coat, old coats from his wardrobe and Mack's—as tightly as he could. Squeezing me into the fifteenth coat often required Zack to literally lift me by the lapels in the dressing room, much to the delight of Mack, who was watching and giggling across the room.

When their routine was over after a fifteen-minute set, they would introduce me with the following: "Some people call him a funny guy with a serious side, some people call him a serious guy with a funny side, but tonight just for and you and you and you—he's going to be (pause for three beats) … "The Rubberband Man." I'm talking about Mr. Bobby Norfolk!!!"

The music DJ "on the box" would cue "The Rubberband Man," and I would stride from the shadows behind the audience into the limelight. Reaching the stage, I began to strip off the fifteen coats to the rhythm of the music. Mack would catch each coat as I tossed it over my head. Meanwhile, Zack chanted "Bobby! Bobby! Bobby!" After the last coat had been tossed, Mack walked backstage as the DJ faded the song. Meanwhile, Zack is still chanting "Bobby! Bobby! Bobby!" I would shoot an incredulous look and deadpan Zack as he did the Temptation Walk off stage, his chant fading. The audience loved it every time, and I hadn't even said a word into the mic yet.

After they had departed the stage, I went into original material through monologs and finished with a poem, either raw or political depending on the energy of the room each particular night. People would see me in the supermarket or the mall and break into, "Bobby! Bobby! Bobby!" while imitating the Temptation Walk. It looked so funny to see what others have been viewing from the audience!

St. Louis music promoters hired us as the opening act for the big name talent that they brought in. We opened for The Jazz Crusaders, Roberta Flack, Peabo Bryson, Ray Goodman & Brown, B.B. King, and Lou Rawls. We were booked to open for Parliament-Funkadelic, Bootsie's Rubberband, and LTD featuring Jeffery Osborne one night. The event was at the Arena Stadium then on Oakland and Hampton Avenue in St. Louis. Zack and Mack were discussing their opening lines when the road manager of LTD started raising the point to those in charge that Bootsie's Rubberband musical equipment had to be taken down so his group could go first. He said LTD had to catch a plane shortly after their set and needed to leave the stadium immediately after performing to get to the airport. The promoters had their stage hands break down Bootsie's equipment and put up LTD's, which meant our act had to be cut to make up for the delay. Despite cutting our act, the experience of being backstage with an All Access Pass was reward enough.

My performance career was on the fast track. I was hobnobbing with big names in entertainment. Throw in my full-time job as an NPS Ranger, and you'd think my plate would be full. But at that time I also began acting with the St. Louis Black Repertory Theatre Company. Mack and I starred in Ron Hime's first production, *The Brownsville Raid*, by Charles Fuller. I later starred in *Zooman* and *The Sign*, also by Charles Fuller. Zack performed with me in the musical *St. Louie' Woman* directed by Kenneth Brown Billups, who had been my mentor in Glee Club at Sumner High and founder of The Legend Singers, an *a cappella* group extraordinaire.

When the theatre was dark, I was a standup comedian, when the theatre season began, I usually worked with the Black Rep half of the season. The NPS job, of course, was my nine-to-five job with pension and benefits.

CHAPTER TWENTY-TWO
Up in Smoke

IN 1977 AT ABOUT ONE in the morning, I was returning from a comedy gig at an East St. Louis nightclub with a huge appetite. The chicken wings served at the bar hadn't appealed to me. For two years, I had "graduated" from all animal flesh—including fish—and was proud of my vegetarian diet. It was working for me. I had hesitated to exclude fish from my diet, I loved it so. However, Big Mack—my comic buddy—would always chide me, "Fish bleed and feel pain, too, brother!" I liked everything from the river and lake: "scum suckers" like catfish and buffalo fish, as well as tuna, salmon, mackerel, sardines, shrimp and scallops from the oceans. The only forms of aquatic life that held no attraction for me were lobster, oysters, and slimy stuff like eels and whale blubber. Well, this particular night I had "a fetish for fish." I seemed to have forgotten the lesson of The Fish Eye a few years earlier.

As I drove home, stomach growling, I remembered that my wife, Cindie, who was not vegetarian, had catfish cutlets in the fridge at home. All I needed to do was fry them. When I arrived at my townhouse apartment at 1:45 a.m. in Ferguson, Missouri, on Canfield Drive, Cindie and our young son, Damon, were upstairs sound asleep. I went to the kitchen and pulled three raw catfish filets from the fridge, slapped our cast iron frying pan onto the burner, and ripped open a bag of flour for breading. The burner was on high under the skillet as I dolloped four large spoonfuls of lumpy, white lard into the black pan and watched it quickly dissolve into grease. The hot grease smelled so good!

Turning my back to the range, I began peeling wrap from the catfish and started breading the catfish cutlets in the flour. While breading my soon-to-be succulent 2 a.m. meal, a loud WHOOSH caught my attention. Twirling around, I saw that the skillet had caught fire! I had set the flame way too high and was now confronted with a grease fire! Immediately, I grabbed the skillet and put it into the sink and ... turned on the cold water.

Science lesson in basic physics: water consumes fire, and the flames are extinguished, yes?

NO! The exception is a grease fire. MUCH later people told me, "You're supposed to smother an oil fire. *Smother* the flames using flour or the skillet lid to deprive the fire of oxygen." Nope, not me. I put cold water on it and BOOM!!! The explosion rang in my ears as heat singed my face, and the concussion knocked me to the floor. I laid there, flat on my back.

The volatile energy of hot cooking grease coming into immediate contact with cold water created a small bomb that threw me flat on my back. My face was burning from the heat of the explosion, and I feared my face was burned off, literally melted from the grease fire. Horrified, I jumped up and ran to the upstairs bathroom mirror. The medical kit was in there, too, and I wanted to see if I was now looking like The Red Skull from the Captain America comic books.

Grasping the sink with both hands, I leaned toward the mirror. Was I prepared to witness the horror that I had inflicted upon myself? I had been driven by a midnight hunger, and had acted in haste. I had been thinking with my stomach. In the mirror, I saw that my face was bright red and glowing, but my skin was still intact. Whew!

Splashing my face with cold water from the sink, I took my first deep breath since the explosion. A soothing relief came over me. I continued splashing cold water on my face until the stinging pain subsided. The mirror confirmed that the bright redness was much less intense on my face. I got some antiseptic burn cream from the cabinet and slathered my face with it. I assumed my wife and kid thought the sound was from outside. They slept through it behind their closed bedroom doors.

Suddenly, I remembered that I left the skillet in the sink with the water running. In another panic, I ran back downstairs and stopped at the last five steps when I saw billowing plumes of thick black smoke drifting through the downstairs. Did I set the house on fire? There were no smoke detectors in the townhouse. I staggered through the columns of black smoke, holding my breath, making my way toward the sink where I heard running water. Twisting the water off, I said a prayer of thanks. There were no flames, just a cloud of thick, black, greasy smoke clinging to the ceiling throughout the downstairs.

I opened the sliding patio door in the kitchen/dining area and immediately the smoke began seeping out into the crisp night air. It was 3 a.m. Then I opened the front door to create a cross-current to get the smoke out faster. After about thirty minutes, with the help of a floor fan, the house was clear of smoke. It was 3:30 a.m. Then I saw that the once beautiful eggshell white walls were now laden with thick, black, greasy smut!

I thought to myself, "This is not good." Assembling cotton rags, sponges, and a bucket of soapy water, I attempted to scrub the walls. My arm-wide sponge arcs revealed not clean walls, but greasy tracks. I had smeared the grease even worse. At 4:15 a.m., I abandoned the failed clean-up effort and went to bed wondering how to fix the situation when daylight came. When my wife and kid woke up hacking and blowing soot into tissues, I confessed to the mess I had made downstairs. They were beyond shocked to see the walls. A trip to the hardware store resulted in sage advice from the guy in the paint department. He explained what chemicals I needed to clean the walls. And he recommended the right paint and brushes to use following the clean-up.

As I toiled off and on over five long days to restore the walls, it gave me time to think: *why would I, a rational vegetarian, do something this insane?* The Universe was clearly saying, "Time to move on."

Like the smoke, it was time to cast my fate to the wind, and cast the fish back into the river. From that day on, fish have remained in the water … and off my plate!

Ahhhh, "the purification of the body temple!"

By 1978, I had been a dedicated vegetarian for three years. No regrets. No late-night longings for ribeyes or Mama's beef roast with carrots, potatoes, and onions. Eating right was an important part of my spiritual regimen. Body, mind, and soul felt at peace. Integration of each aspect of my being was more important to me than any particular flavor or treat.

Later that day, I was to be tested yet again! While driving through Forest Park in metro Saint Louis one hot July day, I made a fateful turn and found myself passing the picnic grounds. People were barbecuing ribs. The smell of hickory smoke and barbecue sauce was powerful. It was so compelling that it took me back to the days when I ate Mom's short ribs as a kid, hunched over the plate scarfing it down. As Oscar Wilde once said, "I can resist everything but temptation."

As I drove out of Forest Park, childhood and young adult memories flooded my mind like Dumbledore's pensive. My brain instructed me to find a building with a smoking shed attached. Ahead, on the same road, I would pass Academy Bar-B-Q, near Sherman Park in the West End of St. Louis. Was it fate? Was it weakness? I wasn't sure that it was anything other than plain, old-fashioned greed. Before I knew it, the car had parked itself at one of the concrete curbs outside, and I was inside, at the order counter. Having given in to temptation, the choice was easy. I ordered a sandwich of short ribs with potato salad, a slice of sweet potato pie and a bottle of red soda pop. There were no other vegetarians to shame me; my fall from determined habit was a private shame.

Oh, did that barbecue sandwich taste good! Sitting on a bench in Sherman Park, chomping into that thick sandwich with sauce dripping between my fingers, I communed with the memories of my early days, my soul food days. Satisfying my fetish for a rib tip sandwich brought back the faces of my parents, brothers, uncles, aunts, and a yard full of cousins. It was *soooo* good! Just like I remembered!

By that evening, however, things turned ugly. My system totally rejected the pork that I had so happily eaten. Mixed with potato salad and sweet potato pie, and washed down with red soda pop, that pork was making a statement in my belly. A Fallen Vegetarian—even for one meal—I heard the sounds of a major gastronomic occurrence! If I wasn't kneeling with my face in the commode, I was sitting on it. The combination of nausea and diarrhea is a powerful physiological lesson. Then a migraine headache set in and would not budge for two days. I was in the throes of withdrawal from barbecue. My system was telling me, *Bobby, you have sinned and fallen short! You dine on swine, and you will pay a fine!* Oh, how I knew it! There was no way around it, no way over it, no way under it. I was destined to live through a three-day "healing crisis."

Back in the day when people got sick like that, I had a comic routine; calling for "Ralph and Earl." We figured that the sound of someone puking down the hall was like "RALPH! EARL!"

That spontaneous indulgence cured me for good. No more did I have the desire to go to the dark side of eating! My habit had been to chew my meal insufficiently before washing it down with red soda pop. Later, I learned the proper way of drinking water—after the meal—and the importance of chewing my food thoroughly before swallowing. This way one avoids gastronomic problems that send one to the medicine cabinet after dinner.

Upper Left—This is the announcement of a tour Dr. Na'im Akbar and I lead to Accra, Ghana West Africa and Cairo, Egypt, in July, 1993.

Lower Right—I met many old friends and made lots of new ones in the Parkhurst Brothers Publishers booth at the American Library Association Conference in Chicago, June 2013.

Right—My life changed forever when my granddaughter, Mikaylah Grace Norfolk, was born. She is a budding actress, model, and scholar.

Below—Here I am dressed in period costume as York, the body servant of William Clark, Co-Captain of The Corps of Discovery. This Living History program, commemorated the bicentennial of Lewis & Clark's voyage from St. Louis to Oregon and back in 1804-06.

Above—The storytelling team of Sherry and Bobby Norfolk, also known around our house as "The Dynamic Duo."

Below—Here I am with my Husky/Shepard mix, Justine, researching a word from the dictionary.

8   The Riverfront Times   July 5, 1979

PEOPLE

Bobby Norfolk— There's a message in this comedian's madness

By Mary Huss

The word comedian generally conjures up an image of a rather loud character—a real attention hound who's always hamming it up and slapping people on the back.

Bobby Norfolk is a comedian who defies that description. He is calm, reserved, almost dignified in his presence, and speaks softly and slowly. By day he's a mild-mannered park ranger at the Old Court-house. But at night he's been known to do such off the wall things as "strip" off the 15 coats he's wearing to the accompaniment of "Rubberband Man."

Norfolk is the founder and main man of the Bobby Norfolk Comedy Revue, a group that has been gaining recognition in the St. Louis area since about 1976. Norfolk and his two cohorts, Zachary Scott Carey and John McHaynes, otherwise known as Zack and Mack, have played to audiences in such places as the Chase Park-Plaza, Cervantes Convention Center and a number of local hotels and nightclubs and currently are making the push for national recognition.

Although the group professes to provide "humor for all occasions," Norfolk says his forte is political satire. His style is reminiscent of that of his idol, Dick Gregory. It's a style that has grown out of his strong interest in human rights and his activity in the peace movement in the sixties.

"Comedy is one of the most powerful mediums for expressing contemporary issues," Norfolk says. "It's a way that people can laugh at their own idiosyncracies and follies, yet think seriously about them when they go home. It's like the proverbial sugar coated pill."

Opening up closed minds is what he really wants to do with his comedy, he says. "I'd like to think that I can help bring some sanity back to America." Although he often works in nightclubs, Norfolk says, "Telling risqué jokes to boozers is not what my comedy is all about. I never want to perform solely for laughs. My main love is college crowds—those concerned with contemporary issues and legitimate creative satire."

College is where the 28-year-old got his start. While a student at Missouri St. Louis in the late seventies he was very active in the peace movement. So how does that figure into comedy? Well, some people were burning things

hell my friends and I would get together and do coffee houses and rap sessions.

These sessions consisted of dramatic poetry readings mixed with some humorous material.

Then he began to get a few breaks. He did some "big shows," like an opening for Lou Rawls on the Admiral, as emcee spot for a concert with three groups at Kiel Auditorium and a warm up session for

Bobby Norfolk wears two hats—that of a park ranger and that of a comedian.

THE BOBBY NORFOLK COMEDY REVUE

Upper left—This article in The Riverfront Times of St. Louis (July, 1979), told of my dual careers as stand-up comedian and NPS Ranger.

Lower right—The Comedy Review: Here I am with fellow funnymen (from left): Zachary Scott Carey, Walter Pritchard, and Johnnie McHaynes.

107

ICMF & KKSS
presents
The Crusaders

with guest **Bobby Norfolk**
Comedian-Political Satirist

CHASE PARK PLAZA HOTEL
ASSAN ROOM
T 9, 1976   7:00 P.M.
NO RESERVE SEA

Above—One of my best gigs was opening for The Jazz Crusaders in an evening of The 1976 Inner City Music Festival, sponsored by radio station KKSS FM.

Left—One of the three Emmys received while performing on the TV show *Gator Tales* on the CBS affiliate Channel 4 in St. Louis, this one received in 1990.

Above—Here I am performing at the UMSL Founder's Dinner Celebration, 2014, held at the Ritz-Carleton in St. Louis. During the ceremonies, I was honored to receive a Distinguished Alumni Award from my alma mater.

Below—This picture was taken atop Mount Bromo, a volcano in East Java, Indonesia (2009). Smaller volcanos are visible in the distance.

Above—Parkhurst Brothers Publishers included me in their booth at the American Library Association Annual Conference in Chicago, June 2013. In this picture, you see me with Ted Parkhurst, a former chairman of the National Storytelling Network, and president of the publishing company.

Below—I am flanked by my parents, Willie and Polly Norfolk.

Above—My mentor, Ms. Jackie Torrence, with "The Three Babas:" Jamal Karam, Kenya Ajanaku, and me, at the St. Louis Festival, 1995. This photo was taken by a festival attendee.

Left—This cover for the *St. Louis Sun TV Week* magazine shows me and Doug Kincaid's Grouchie Gator. Aaron Mermelstein was the photographer and reporter (1988).

111

Above—At the Anchorage, Alaska Zoo, I was upstaged by Maggie, a three-ton pachyderm, who shared her treat —a dandelion— with me as I was telling stories to a teen audience (2000).

Right—Look closely and you will see me repelling off a cliff wall at Shoshone Point, in the Grand Canyon (1983) This photo was taken by the Chief Ranger of Grand Canyon National Park.

Right—This 1983 show bill promoted a dressy New Year's Eve gig at which Bobby Norfolk's Comedy Review (featuring my buddies Zack and Mack) was headlined.

Below—My Eighth Grade graduating class at Riddick School in St. Louis, 1965; Look for me in the second row from the top, third from the right.

FOLKS PRODUCTIONS
PRESENTS

A NIGHT IN HOLLYWOOD

STARRING: **BOBBY NORFOLK'S COMEDY REVUE**
featuring the Comedy Team of **ZACK & MACK**

SPECIAL GUEST STARS
THE FABULOUS LASHAYS

M.C.'s AL RICHARDSON &
JUNIOR • THE UNPREDICTED

Your Musical Host: A. FRANK

Help bring in the New Year The Old Way!
DATE: Sat., Jan. 1, 1983
TIME: 8:00 P.M.-1:00 A.M.
PLACE: HOLLYWOOD NIGHTS
9765 St. Charles Rock Rd.
DONATION: $3 in adv./$5 at door

A Special Presentation To
St. Louis Social Productions
& Promotional Organizations
MR. BERNIE HAYES
Presenter of Awards
Breakaway Unlimited • Chez Ce Soir
Dollar Bill • Friends • Hart To Hart
J.R.L.W. • Rainbow • R.E.F.
Regal Sports • Renaissance

CHAPTER TWENTY-THREE

Call 911

IN 1979, A NEIGHBOR friend of mine asked me to try something he called "power boost pills." He claimed the pills would give me a joyful burst of energy, increase my brain power, and make me more "dynamic" at parties and other social settings. I swallowed the pills without questioning what he was offering me. Later, I would wish I'd asked him about its origin. My experience during the first hours after taking the pills was that my neighbor was right. That evening I felt all of the things he said: amazing, powerful, electrified, and electrifying. Already buffed from my strict dietary regimen, gym workout schedule and martial arts classes, I now felt positively indestructible.

Feeling so energized, I went into the basement of my house and started lifting weights and doing push-ups. I felt invincible!

Then it happened. My first awareness was that my heart was suddenly beating several times faster than normal. As I sat on the bench in the workout area, I tried to figure why my heart just got so over-active. The racing of my heart was unknown in my life experiences—a first. I knew the heart is operated by the autonomic nervous system and beats at a certain rate per minute according to one's activity. I thought. "Okay, you overdid it with the exercise, so relax." But my heart would not relax. In fact, it then shot up to an alarming rate. My next awareness was that I was hyperventilating.

Remembering that my wife and young son were upstairs

watching television, I rushed through the hall, out of the back door into the yard. My anxiety increased along with my heart rate until it felt like my chest would explode at any moment. I crawled under a line of bushes behind the house and thought, If I lay face down in the dirt I will die silently and not be seen in the back yard the next morning. I suddenly felt a soft white light over my back. I lifted my head slightly and saw the white light reflected on the ground. I stared at the reflection and sensed a presence over the bush and myself.

A voice inside my head spoke, "You will be fine, but will have to suffer a little more to learn the lesson."

Suddenly the warmth of the light and the glow was gone. I sat up in the night, cross-legged in the grass and back to normal. Standing up, lifting my face to the sky, I started praising my return to normalcy. Then, a few seconds later, I felt the full force of the words of the lesson I had felt being spoken to. The revelation came to pass as my heart started racing faster than ever and again panic set in. Somehow, I had the clarity to run inside the house and tell Cindie to call 911. I was having a heart attack, I told her. She rushed to comfort me. As she reached me, I suddenly envisioned myself in a coffin. With renewed urgency, I urged her to call an ambulance. As she ran to the phone, I staggered into the front yard. The ground came up to meet me as I slumped outside the door, then I turned face-up and waited, gasping for breath.

Just minutes later, the ambulance rolled to a stop right in front of my house. Paramedics jumped out, stretcher clanking, and loaded me in the back. Then the race to the hospital began. I felt I was hovering above my body in the back of the ambulance as it heeled while taking corners on the way to the Emergency Room. I saw the ambulance roar up to the ER's double doors, three paramedics leapt from the ambulance, and carted me inside on a stretcher. A rubbery-smelling oxygen mask slowed my heart rate. I was immediately admitted to the Intensive Care Unit (ICU). Blood and urine tests were ordered right away to explain my condition. The tests found nothing. No traces of poisons or stimulants of any kind were evident in my system. Baffled by their usually-reliable tests, the doctors were stumped as was I. "That's strange," the men and women in white coats agreed.

Later, when my neighbor muttered into my ear, "It never had that effect on me," I too was baffled at what had caused my near-heart attack.

The medical staff having all been stupefied on what happened to me, released me twenty-four hours later with a heart monitor strapped to my chest and waist. I was instructed to wear it twenty-four hours a day—full-time, except when showering. The monitor recorded my heart rate as I moved from sedentary to strenuous activity, giving the doctors a view into my daily activities. I wore it under my National Parks Service uniform. I felt like some kind of robot with this machine hooked to me. Numb, I walked to work, feeling like a bizarre extension of myself. For more than a week, the monitor was my constant companion throughout every aspect of my daily schedule. After ten days, the doctors saw no unusual rate fluctuations in my heart, and I gave them their monitor back.

A fellow park service ranger wanted me to be one of his groomsmen for his wedding shortly after that. Morris and I hung out together infrequently outside of work, but he did the groomsman thing because I was a co-worker. I rented a tuxedo for the wedding with the trauma still fresh in my mind. We rangers are a close-knit group and I was determined to honor his request by participating. In the photos he shared with me later, I could see the dour look of seriousness on my face in contrast to the grinning bridesmaid I escorted. I seemed to be thinking, "I almost didn't make the wedding, but a Higher Power told me I'd be fine."

CHAPTER TWENTY-FOUR

Python in the Night Club

DURING MY YEARS DOING STAND-UP comedy in nightclubs, I fell victim to the desire to freshen up my routine, to "spice up my act," as it were. Every performer wants to surprise his audience from time to time, and I figured out how to do so in an unforgettable way! It was the opening of the act that I felt needed some pizzazz. A friend knew I was in need, and he proved a friend indeed!

The friend in question was a co-worker with me at the Gateway Arch. His pet was an eight-foot Amazon python. After thinking about how to broach the subject, I asked him if I could use his snake in my opening for just one night. Friend that he was, he thought it was a delightful idea. So one evening, we drove to his house after work and I made a new acquaintance ... a flesh-eating, eight-foot serpent. A scaly monster weighing in at eighty-three pounds.

I watched as my friend fed the python a dead rat. After all, she should have a full belly before I handled her. That was not a very pleasant sight, I tell you.

After its luscious meal, he put the python around my neck. The weight of that thing was like having a truck tire around my neck. A live truck tire!

Fortunately, the python did not consider me dessert. After ninety minutes or so, I finally got used to the contraction of her body moving around my neck, over my arms, *and wherever she very well pleased!*

Perhaps you could call what we did bonding. The lady python relaxed as I felt the lump of a rat inside the python's body, making its slow descent down her digestive tract.

The next night, my friend brought the python to the nightclub in a canvas sack. When we settled ourselves backstage, the python and I reacquainted ourselves. I had chosen a white-hooded robe for dramatic effect. My intent was to appear like a Merlin type of mystic who commands beasts of the animal kingdom. The unsuspecting audience was seated at dining tables about six feet from the slightly elevated stage. After the emcee announced my name, I appeared from behind the curtain. Here I was, a standup comic, bedecked in a blinding white robe ... with the slithering creature around my neck!

The audience in the front section was obviously unaware that I would be so audacious as to bring a live eight-foot python into their midst. Their orientation was insufficient, perhaps accounting for the communal gasp audible from the parking lot.

Yes, my well-intentioned plan went awry.

The hot dates in little black dresses failed to appreciate my extraordinary preparation for their amusement.

When the python raised her head and licked at the air, sniffing the room, the front tables realized they were being presented with—not the usual standup one-liners—but a line that was eight feet long and a *live snake!* The audience reacted as if I had drawn a weapon! Jumping up from their seats, men and women alike knocked over their tables, spilling drinks, kicked their chairs—and many of their neighbors—trying to exit the building!

I saw a swath created, the biggest tippers departing the fastest, as man after woman cleared the room. Patrons in the middle and back—not the best tippers—were alerted as the first rows yelled, "He has a python on stage, and it's *alive!*"

I mean, it wasn't like the snake had legs and was going to chase them out of the building.

Assessing the situation like a true professional, I quickly unwound my friend's pet from my neck and arms and handed it off backstage. Then I pulled off the luminous white robe and addressed my rattled audience. The club owner was not amused either and urged me to quickly tell some jokes! However, as word flowed through the crowd that the snake was retired, order was restored in the room.

As I finished my comedy routine, I made a mental note not ever to try that little act again. My improv was making fun of those hearty patrons who remained in their seats, nervously checking me out for further carnivores. Seeing none, they slowly picked up the scattered tables and chairs and sat back down. "You big babies! Afraid of an eight-foot snake ..." Some—those in the front rows returned warily. The audience in the back thought it was hilarious.

One night we had a gig in East St. Louis. I was disillusioned with the night club scene. I'd had enough of the smoky rooms, the assumption that everyone was into booze and narcotics, the staying up until 2 or 3 a.m. to be paid after all the drawers from the wait staff were turned in and counted. I physically could not get up, cross the room and go to the gig. I called in sick and asked Zack and Mack to do the gig. They weren't pleased by my sudden resignation, but they continued the club work without me. With remarkable endurance and discipline, Zack and Mack worked the Funny Bone Comedy Clubs and East St. Louis clubs to the point they became a singular act. They established their independence.

With time on my hands to work on my craft, I studied other performers, planning to improve my storytelling ability and to hone my stagecraft. My determination was to take it to the next level.

During this time, I studied the genius of two individuals who I call "The Two Michaels"—Michael Jackson and Michael Jordan.

The musical Michael had a stage presence that I wanted to emulate in my own way. When he combined vocals and dance, then added unique musical arrangements, he was way beyond Elvis or Springsteen—the King and the Boss. Using his form of stagecraft, the athlete Michael took his game (and the Chicago Bulls) to heights unimagined. The commercial affirmation of his star status was confirmed—another kind of "heights"—when his personal brand became ubiquitous. The acclaimed "Air Jordan" was all over television, magazines, and other media. While I never expected to achieve the universal acclaim of The Two Michaels, I was determined to be the best I could be.

The more I got involved in traditional storytelling, the more Zack and Mack wondered what I was up to. They just could not understand the concept. I'm not sure I fully understood performance storytelling at that time either, but it's where my strong intuition was leading me. Zack and Mack decided finally to pull up stakes in St. Louis and head for New York City, Mecca for those seeking "the big time." As a musical mentor, Oliver Sain, told me one night, "Bobby, you have to go West over the Rockies or East over the Appalachians. Every now and then, you have to get out of the valley of St. Louis."

The parting was difficult. Zack and Mack really wanted me to go with them. I had my young son and wife, my National Park Service job and "this new thing called Storytelling." All of those values made it clear I must say no to my longtime friends. They were frustrated, even angry and rude to me at times.

As the months passed, I received postcards from Zack and Mack as their national travels took them from New York City to Toronto, Canada, and on to Los Angeles and Phoenix. I was proud of them;

they were on their way to the top. They appeared on TV on *The Redd Foxx Show* and *Sesame Street*, and in a B-movie called *Nice Girls Don't Explode*.

One day, Zack wasn't feeling right. Mack took him to the hospital for tests. Zack's legs were badly swollen. His organs were not getting enough blood. He called me out of the blue one night and said he wasn't angry with me anymore or frustrated about my decision. He said he respected me. He asked for forgiveness for any rudeness in the past. We chatted for ten or fifteen minutes before saying goodnight. A week later, Zack, Mack, and their Roadie, Big Mike, were traveling on the New Jersey Turnpike. Zack, who usually loved to drive, asked Big Mike to take the wheel. Zack said he would rest in the back of the van. An hour later, Mike and Mack heard Zack wheezing. His bulk was gyrating the entire van. Zack's 500-pound frame shook violently. In a moment, he was gone by a massive heart attack. Three years later, Mack followed with congestive heart failure at Veteran's Administration Hospital on Grand Boulevard in St. Louis.

CHAPTER TWENTY-FIVE

The Black Repertory Company of St. Louis

EVER SINCE MY GRADE SCHOOL DISCOVERY of the joy of performance art, I have felt a powerful spiritual force at work when on stage. There is a unique triangulation of creativity, communication, and human interaction when the awareness of playwright, performing troupe, and audience come together at a particular moment in time. That power is stronger than anything that can be captured on film, broadcast, on TV, or pressed into a video disc. Live performance varies from moment to moment, from performance to performance. The nuances of a playwright's words, the way those nuances are expressed in the voices and bodily movements of actors, together with the unmistakable contribution made by the "Oooohs," "Aaaaahs," laughter—and even silences—of a live audience comprise an existential moment in time. That moment is a point on the continuum of art and a moment in the spiritual life of each one involved. I feel it every time the curtain goes up.

The productions that I have been fortunate to do with the Black Repertory Theatre of St. Louis (the Black Rep), have all been strong evocations of that artistic learning experience. They began, for me, in 1981, when Ron Himes cast me to perform in *The Brownsville Raid*. The play was set in Brownsville, Texas. In the play, a platoon of African-American soldiers is accused of a killing after they had been taunted and harassed by the local population. The play was based on actual events during the administration of Teddy Roosevelt. The energy brought by each person in the theatre, whether on-stage, backstage, or in the audiences, combined for memorable evenings.

My personal favorite of all the productions I have performed in at the Black Rep remains *The Wiz*. It has been my good fortune and delight to have been cast in two characters by Ron for the Rep's productions of that remarkable play. One role was the Head Underling for Evillene, the Wicked Witch. The other character I was selected to play was the Royal Gate Keeper of Oz.

These roles allowed me to employ many of the artistic techniques I had learned over the years. As the Head Underling, Evillene has a song "Don't Bring Me No Bad News." Well, I was the one bringing the bad news. My gymnastics training came in handy every time Evillene gave me a wave of her hand and arm. An "invisible force" would knock me over, tumbling from one end of the stage to the next. The audience reaction to these acrobatics gave me more energy and satisfaction than, I think, could ever be communicated to anyone who has not acted on stage.

As the Royal Gatekeeper, I drew inspiration from George Clinton of Parliament-Funkadelic. I had a huge bright green Afro wig on, matching cape, sequined green hip boots, Elton John-type sunglasses—"Bennie and the Jets"—bare-chested under the cape, and sequenced green tight shorts. The character I portrayed was how I thought Richard Pryor would do the Royal Gatekeeper.

The audience loved it. Even Dorothy, the Tin Man, the Scarecrow, and the Cowardly Lion were suppressing laughter and were glad that their backs were to the audience as I delivered my lines.

CHAPTER TWENTY-SIX

The Mountain Goat in Me

WHILE A SENIOR AT UMSL, I was approached by a friend who had been asked to apply for a summer job at the Gateway Arch in downtown St. Louis. Eric, my friend, was not interested because he was applying for prelaw school and asked me if I wanted to apply. I thought, *Why not?* The Danforth Foundation money had been spent and a new source of steady income would be welcome.

It was now 1976 and I was disillusioned by most events in America. Things seemed to be going downhill for black people. Many African-American leaders had been seduced into figurehead roles in mainstream businesses. Some sought voluntary exile, as Eldridge

Cleaver did. Some were imprisoned. As some disappeared from the scene, there were claims that many were threatened with imprisonment, and some were actually killed. This all came to light when the Freedom of Information Act was employed to reveal the activities of COINTELPRO. In this time and atmosphere, there was clearly a distrust between the government and many Americans.

During the Carter Administration, fully-laden gasoline tankers were moored off U.S. ports because of an oil embargo by OPEC and the seven major American oil companies: Exxon, Amoco, Gulf, Shell, Texaco, Phillips, and Sinclair. People languished in gasoline lines for an hour or more to get only ten gallons—or less—of rationed gasoline. Prices soared from twenty-five cents in 1970 to the insane price of sixty-four cents! Imagine that!

Meanwhile, I went to the Arch for my interview with Chief Ranger Dan Murphy. Before that day, I thought the Arch and its administrative building, the Old Court House where the Dredd Scott Trial began, was a city-run facility. My first exposure to the National Park Service was an eye-opening event. Sure, I had watched the 630-foot stainless steel structure of the Gateway Arch being built during my middle school years from the third-floor window of my homeroom at Riddick School at Evans and Sarah Streets. The "tiny legs and creeper cranes" were visible five miles away. Before I met Ranger Murphy, that was the extent of my connection with the NPS.

As Ranger Murphy interviewed me, he asked several questions about government, politics, philosophy, and history. I must have aced the interview because he asked if I could start the next day! I stammered that I had accepted a two-week job at a summer camp at Lake of the Ozarks a week ago.

He countered, "Can you start the Monday after you get back?"

"Yes," was my reply. I left there with my head spinning. I had never been to the Arch until that day. Upon arrival, I found out it was a national park site. Knowing I was going to be working for the federal government that I maligned during my college years, was almost too much to take in. Talk about coming full circle! It was not different than the antiwar protesters and hippies who, after college, put on Brooks Brothers suits and went to work in their fathers' businesses. The James Bond wannabe would be wearing the green uniform of the National Park Service. That other side of my youthful persona, the country bumpkin, would now be working in one of the sleekest structures in America, in the heart of a major metropolis.

Awaking the next morning, I could not help thinking of the white concept of the "Young Urban Professional." I thought of how that newsworthy slice of society contrasted with my peers, young African-Americans. Both groups were successfully accommodating themselves to living in rapidly-changing urban areas, but the contrasts were often stark. Those young blacks were sometimes called "Buppies" (Black Urban Professionals). For sociological purposes, it looked like distinctions had to be made. On a personal level, my transition from a black militant to a uniformed officer of "the establishment" made it suddenly clear to me that I was coming-of-age in a uniquely evolving society. I realized that, just as my ambitions to change the world by cunning and force (as the next James Bond) may have been unrealistic, America and I were changing from within.

The first of my ranger training sessions was in Harper's Ferry, West Virginia, in 1978. A fellow National Park ranger and I took a plane from St. Louis to Washington, D.C. It was my very first flight. I was the first person in my immediate family to fly in an airplane. I was excited beyond belief. It was late April and the cherry blossoms were in bloom on the Capitol Mall. I had never seen pink trees before. As the plane glided over the Washington airspace, I witnessed a visual extravaganza of cherry trees in bloom, outlining the monuments, the White House, the Capitol, and the Smithsonian museums. Everywhere I looked, the cherry blossoms seemed to frame the city in a pink cloud. We toured the monuments all day, then boarded an evening train into the Stephen T. Mather Training Center at Harper's Ferry. Harper's Ferry is famous for a few reasons. Explorer Meriwether Lewis went to the military depot there in 1803 to obtain military supplies for the Corps of Discovery that would explore from St. Louis to Oregon. Half a century later, abolitionist John Brown laid siege to Harper's Ferry in 1859. John Brown's rebellion was put down by United States troops led by none other than Robert E. Lee, who later led the Confederate forces against the Union Army during the United States Civil War.

Park ranger training included a variety of topics, from the history of the national park system to daily duties interacting with the public at park sites. Because park rangers sometimes double as docents, we were given one session on telling the story of our park's history and resources. That was where I saw truly professional storytellers for the first time ever. One morning in a class called Basic Interpretive Skills, a duo named "The Folk Tellers" presented a workshop on storytelling skills we might use as park rangers. The class was led by two storytellers, Barbara Freeman and Connie Reagan Blake. I thought, *what a very creative and imaginative way to make a living, and they are fantastic!*

On the first weekend, we rangers were free to roam anywhere we wanted from five o'clock Friday evening to eight o'clock Monday morning. Saturday morning after breakfast, I decided to hike the bluffs of the Appalachian Mountains that towered around us. While I had never hiked in mountains in my life, I figured it looked easy. I also didn't know about defined trails, trail heads, or footpaths. Seeing a mountainside that seemed to have enough low growth for me to grab onto, I found a hiking stick and *up like Spiderman I went.* Occasionally I would look back. The road below got smaller and smaller. Passing cars got tinier and tinier. After reaching the summit, I stood on an overhanging rock to look at the vista.

The Potomac and Shenandoah Rivers have their confluence at Harper's Ferry. I could see clearly for several miles up each river valley. The climb and the early hour had made me sleepy, so I laid down on the flat rock to take a nap in the warm April sun. I awoke in a fetal position, totally disoriented. It took my mind several minutes to process my location. I felt the rock under me, I felt the sun and breeze on me, but I was clueless as to my location. When I sat up, I saw that not far from me stood a buzzard, staring at me. I thought, *This bird thinks I'm carrion for his breakfast.* He was ready to peck my bones until I sat up and we were both surprised. He flew off in search of a more passive meal.

When I decided to descend the mountain, I was shocked to realize that this mountain slope was very, very steep. I had never descended a steep slope before. Questions arose. Should I go backward or forward? Forward looked like the best option, so I grabbed tree after tree trying not to exceed a manageable speed. Maintaining my footing was critical. When no trees were in reach, I sat and scooted down the slope with both hands behind me. It was grueling and challenging, but I reached the road again. Feeling a great sense of accomplishment, I walked back to the apartment. I had scaled my first mountain totally by instinct, daring, and some primal skill that I dredged up in the survival reservoir of my brain. In other words, I didn't have a clue what I was doing, but thoroughly enjoyed the effort.

A fellow ranger did reprimand me for my failure to tell anyone where I was going. In case I had an accident, it would be important for someone to know where to look before the buzzard got me for real. My first lesson in being a skilled ranger was learned that day.

Occasionally, the National Park Service sent selected rangers away for further training. In the spring of 1983, I was assigned to a course called "Ranger Skills" on the South Rim of the Grand Canyon in Arizona. My chief ranger at the Gateway Arch in St. Louis said, "As soon as you get a chance after you get settled in your living quarters, walk the twenty-minute road to the rim. Stand with your feet planted firmly and look into The Hole—The Resource. It will set the tone for the next six weeks."

We flew from St. Louis to Phoenix, Arizona, and then took a connecting flight to the airport at the Canyon. Park rangers greeted thirty-five of us in government vans that whisked us in a caravan to Albright Training Center. After settling into my apartment, I had the rest of the afternoon to explore on my own. Following the recommendation of my boss in St. Louis, I walked the quarter mile to the Bright Angel Trailhead on the South Rim. There, I first explored a fabulous restaurant called the El-Tovar. It was recommended that we have a few meals there during our six-week stay to savor the exquisite meals and take in the ambiance of the Lodge-Pole Pine architecture. What I saw when I walked past the El-Tovar was a striated red wall in the distance. That wall turned out to be the North Rim, twenty-six miles across the Canyon. The sight was breathtaking, the word "surreal" comes to mind.

I walked gingerly to the edge of the South Rim and planted my feet firmly on the ground before looking down, *and I do mean down!* The sight immediately took me aback. I gasped, blinked, and my eyes grew large. I gasped again and wondered if I was looking at a massive abstract painting. Looking down, I saw a switchback trail, which I suspected would be the Bright Angel Trail. The trail wound into a massive hole with a serpentine "tail" at a distant point. That "tail" turned out to be the Colorado River, and it was outlined by what I thought were little bushes. Later, it was explained to me that most all of those "bushes" were 200 feet tall and called Ponderosa pines. Some were smaller pinyon and juniper pines. About two-thirds of the way down, the trail led to a campground called Indian Gardens. The trail then dove into the Colorado River, which looked like a crack in the sidewalk from this distance. That "crack in the sidewalk" was moving very swiftly. Foaming rapids rushed through the Grand Canyon, visible even from my 5,000-foot vantage point on the rim above. That seemingly tiny river, over two billion years, had given the canyon its form.

The Grand Canyon is "one of the jewels in the crown" of the National Park System. However, humans have cherished its beauty for thousands of years. I was standing on ground held sacred for centuries by the indigenous peoples of that area, the Navajo, Hopi, Havasupai, and Yavapai people.

Our Ranger Skills course started with a week of orientation. Lecturers explained the science and folklore of the Canyon, including the forces that had formed it billions of years ago. We learned about its flora and fauna, and were surprised to learn that many species living there could be found nowhere else on the planet. The second week we were taught interpretive techniques to use in our respective National Park sites. Our thirty-five-member group represented a diverse cross section of the National Park System. The third week we were taught methods for search and rescue, which varied with the sites and geography of each park. The fourth week was devoted to firefighting.

Firefighting seemed hypothetical to a ranger who spent his days around a stainless steel structure beside the Mississippi River, but it was anything but hypothetical in parks like the Grand Canyon, which includes native forests. We learned to dig a firebreak in the rocky ground to create a trench that would, it was hoped, stop or slow down an encroaching forest or grass fire. These exercises were grueling. I knew that, in real forest fire conditions, the work would be incredibly dangerous. Imagining flames burning thousands of acres of trees and brush per hour, combined with inhaling smoke day in and day out, I was struck with awe for the teams that fight fires as a primary task. Those men and women routinely go "in harm's way" as certainly as any infantry personnel.

The sixth week, eight of us descended into the depths of the Grand Canyon carrying forty-pound backpacks under the careful watch of our chief ranger. For three days and two nights, we followed the switchbacks of the Bright Angel Trail. Our mission was to reach the Colorado River on the desert floor, cross over it on boulders at one of its small tributaries, continue across the Arizona desert on the Hermit's Loop Trail, then ascend on the third day up the "Red Wall," back to the summit of the South Rim. We had to practice boiling water and sifting out the silt and sand through a square of muslin or cheesecloth. That would be our only source of clean drinking water. Boiling killed the microscopic parasite *giardia* that wreaks havoc on a person's intestinal tract if ingested.

I prepared for the hike by walking down the Bright Angel Trail to Indian Gardens Ranch on three different occasions. It took me three hours down and five hours back to complete the trip. Mules could take tourists down the same trail, but rangers were not allowed to ride mules. We "hardy souls" had to walk!

In the mornings before we went to classes, we would awake to cold temperatures and snow. By afternoon, the snow would melt as the desert temperatures rose to eighty degrees or higher. Each morning we were wearing winter clothes, and by one o'clock they had been replaced with short-sleeved shirts and shorts!

Hiking down the Bright Angel Trail in mid-May when the legendary dry heat of Arizona rose to oven-like temperatures was trial enough. But following twelve horse-sized mules down that trail was double jeopardy. Those mules dropped dung obstacles on the trail, polluting the air when it baked in the dry heat. Along came unwary hikers like me, puffing and panting. The trail was already dusty, the air stagnant in the midday heat—temperatures often reaching ninety-five degrees—and now we had to contend with the aroma of baking mule dung. Gag!

The pull of gravity made it less difficult to descend into the Canyon as opposed to climbing out. Five hours of pulling oneself up from the depths of the Grand Canyon was a test for the soul! I made three practice trips over two weekends to get myself in shape. Be aware that Indian Gardens Ranch is not the entire way down to the Colorado River. The river is still several miles below, as the trail twists and turns.

On the actual hike, a female ranger wore a Gucci hat to shade her face from the sun. The rest of us wore NPS issue baseball caps. At one overlook, the woman was peering over the edge when a sudden gust of wind snatched her expensive hat off her head and hurled it into the abyss. She screamed and reached for it, but the wind was master. We watched in amazement, she in horror, as the Gucci disappeared into nothingness. She cried like a baby.

We were told we could only bring enough water in our canteens for two days. The third day was the boiling/muslin cloth project. It actually worked! None of the thirty-five rangers became ill. One night we slept under the brilliant light of a full moon. The reflection was so intense that we did not need a campfire to see at night around the camp circle. We ate our dinner provisions, which did not require cooking, and got into our sleeping bags to retire for the evening. All night long, the moonlight shone so brightly that it lit up the surrounding mesas and the desert floor.

At one point, we had to rappel off a rock cliff, a sheer rock wall. We strapped climbing ropes and carabiners to personal harnesses and tentatively walked backward off a cliff onto the perpendicular rock wall below. No other situation I have encountered in my life has been more disorienting than dangling in mid-air from a single rope, with nothing below but solid rock, and that dangerously far below. My whole sense of the universe was thrown off as I walked backward down that vertical wall at Shoshoni Point. When my feet first reached the edge of the cliff and the chief ranger said, "All right Norfolk, flex your knees and walk down the cliff wall," I did so on faith. Looking up, I saw blue sky and realized I was standing with my back parallel to the ground—way below. I felt an adrenaline rush that made my heart race. Another guy in our group was told to rappel, but when his feet got to the cliff wall, he began to shake and quake. His entire body vibrated so fast that I thought he was going to burst. He yelled out, "Chief, I can't do it! I can't do it!" The chief ranger hauled him back up.

In spite of the fact that I was out-paced by the longer-legged and more experienced hikers in the group, when we got to the inclines I would always find myself ten to fifteen minutes ahead of the group. When the stragglers arrived at a summit, they would find me already fully rested, relaxed, and breathing easy. My rest period was twice as long as the others. The chief ranger on our hike, J.T. Reynolds, gave me a nickname, "the Barn Burner." He also said my secret was that I ate hay for my energy! I told him it all came down to proper diet, sleep, exercise, breathing, and mental attitude, basics structures of life taught by Yogis and Shamans the world over.

We all made it back to Albright Training Center on the afternoon of the third day. We were so exhausted, our simple apartments seemed like a four-star hotel, but we hadn't lost one person in the ordeal. It had been a training ordeal worthy of a future James Bond, and I had passed. In fact, I thought it was exhilarating and exciting to the maximum degree.

A few days later, we were back in the classroom after lunch when a fellow ranger entered, thirty minutes late. He seemed rattled and was clearly in a strange mood. His eyes seemed to say that he had seen a ghost. Apologizing to the instructor when he came into class, he said he had gone to the Bright Angel Café for lunch and as he ate, he watched dark clouds forming over the Canyon. He went out to the rim to watch. He said the storm grew more intense. Lightning flashed through the black clouds. He saw lightning bolts form in those clouds and make branch-like streaks that struck the canyon floor as he looked *down* at the top of that "black electrical sea!" To see this phenomenon from above, while standing on the earth, and not in an airplane, was magical to him and all who heard his story.

One evening after work at the Arch, Morris, my newlywed African-American co-worker, planned to meet up with several fellow rangers for dinner and a beer at a pub nearby on South Broadway. In the locker room, we changed out of our ranger uniforms, put our "Smokey" hats on the rack, and left work. As we walked the quarter mile to our garage, jovially recruiting other rangers to join us in the after-work outing, we were joined by our white female co-worker, Jan Dolan, and her brother John, who had come to pick her up from work.

John said he would drive us all to the pub and after dinner, he would double back to take Morris and me to our cars. At the base of Washington Avenue near First Street, John pulled his car up and we started the musical chairs bit of who would sit where. I was outside the car with Morris and Jan when traffic behind us started backing up. I urged everyone to "get in the car—anywhere!" We ushered Jan in the front with her brother and Morris and I jumped in the back seat as John zoomed off to the pub. We arrived a few minutes later and found a parking spot near the front door. After a great time eating, drinking, and laughing, Jan went home with another female ranger. John, Morris, and I left to retrieve our cars at our garage. As John started to pull away from the curb, an unmarked police car backed up to our front bumper. Two other cars came out of nowhere with lights and sirens blazing, pinning us in place at an angle from the curb. Cops jumped out of the cars, guns drawn. The biggest one demanded, "Get out the fu—ing car and keep your hands visible where we can see them!"

In shock, John put his car in park, leaving the motor running. All three of us obeyed by stepping gingerly out of the car. From an alley across the street, a television news team rushed in. A well-known reporter led the way. His cameraman sprinted to keep up.

"Put your hands on the fu—ing car and straddle—all three of you—now!" a white cop demanded. In our shock, we obeyed.

Overcoming disbelief, we asked, "What is going on here?" What's this all about?"

"Where's the girl you abducted on First Street?" One of the cops yelled.

"What … girl?" Morris stammered.

"We had a report that two black males abducted a young white female near the Arch!"

John looked over his shoulder and stammered, "That was my

sister! She went home with a friend of hers, and these guys with me are National Park Service rangers!"

Neither the police nor the TV guys believed John, since we were not in uniform. We had changed in the Arch locker room so we could blend in with the other clientele at the pub. The commanding officer ordered us patted down, which included roughly pulling our wallets. After examining our wallets the cops saw … oops NPS rangers indeed, complete with IDs and badges.

One cop called Dispatch from his car, asking that they run a check on all three of us. Several minutes later the cop returned from his car and ordered his team to "stand down," as we were in fact federal rangers. Although he never admitted it, the lead cop's facial expression made it clear that they had made a serious tactical error. Taking all too seriously an uncorroborated report from an unknown driver behind John's car who reported seeing "two black males abduct a white female" had caused them to get egg on their faces. They must have trailed us to the pub and called the police with John's license number and car make. They did not see John "the white guy" who was in the driver's seat.

Now appearing dumbstruck, the police returned our wallets, apologized for our "inconvenience," as the TV crew folded up their equipment, obviously disappointed at the loss of an expected "police action scoop" for the nightly news.

Still shell shocked, John drove us back to the garage, all of us in total silence. No longer scared, we now felt outrage and humiliation settling in. In later years, we would have understood that we'd been victims of racial profiling. Back in the day, we just knew that we'd experienced another installment of the cost of being black in America. That's the lesson we took away from what should have been a quiet evening of well-earned relaxation after a shift serving visitors at the Arch.

CHAPTER TWENTY-SEVEN

My Dinner With John John

A CLASSIC CELEBRITY ENCOUNTER happened on a later trip to The Grand Canyon National Park.

I was invited to return to the Grand Canyon National Park two more times to train park rangers in storytelling and interpretive techniques. This was so rewarding for me because I was now an instructor and not the student. No longer that shy stutterer of my high school days, I cherished recognition as a leader and guide of my adult peers.

One night I went to the El Tovar Restaurant for dinner. While waiting for my reservation for one, I waited in the lobby of the hotel for my name to be called. Standing there, I saw a man browsing in the gift shop, a man whose posture and appearance seemed to command attention. After making his purchase at the register, the man walked out and began conversing with another man who I noticed was wearing a Yale University sweatshirt. My intuition heightened as I saw the guy leave the gift shop. He was broad-shouldered, strode as if he owned the place, and his wavy black hair bespoke power and authority.

Suddenly, the air became slightly "electric" with the premonition that I was in the presence of greatness. I felt I should know his name, but I had yet to see his face full-on. As I fidgeted, waiting for my table, the maître d' called on the intercom, "Table for two, John F. Kennedy Jr."

Wow! I thought. *That's who that is!* I watched as he and his dining companion were escorted into the restaurant. The guy in the Yale shirt was John's best friend, William Sylvester Noonan, who later wrote about his years hanging out with JFK Jr. as a friend and confidant.

Not more than five minutes later my name was called. The server seated me directly across the aisle from JFK Jr. and the other guy. I thought, *This is unreal!* The only way to keep my composure seemed to be to pretend that I was dining with them. John asked our waiter if he could recommend a wilderness trail that he and his friend could go on, one where they would encounter the least number of other hikers. The waiter suggested the Hermit's Loop. I thought, *That's the trail we had to endure on my three-day trip into the Canyon desert.*

I thought, *Why does this national treasure want to go into a dangerous situation with only one other person?* Later, I learned that John F. Kennedy Jr. loved living life on the edge and flirting with danger. When his soup was placed before him, he shook out his napkin and raised his spoon. Then, as I watched on in awe, John F. Kennedy Jr. actually leaned over and slurped it! I chuckled to myself, thinking Jackie Kennedy Onassis would not approve of her son's table manners.

We "dined together" from soup to salad, entrée to dessert. There was no way I was going to leave first. I slowly sipped on my hot tea until, finally, my two unofficial dinner partners rose to leave. While I wanted to caution the son of the late president about the peril of the trail recommended, I held my tongue. Over the years, I had learned to leave celebrities alone when they are in an informal situation like this. Even my hint of notoriety has taught me that performers and others "in the limelight" appreciate privacy every once in a while.

Years later I was saddened deeply when the news came out that

JFK Jr., his wife, and her sister crashed in Kennedy's private plane into the ocean en route to Martha's Vineyard. My mind went back to art class in sixth grade at Turner Middle School in St. Louis. On Nov. 22, 1963, at 1:30 p.m., the principal came on the intercom to announce that an assassin in Dallas, Texas, had killed President John F. Kennedy. Later, during the funeral, JFK's son, three-year-old John John, walked out from Jackie Kennedy's side to salute his dad's casket on national television.

The closest thing we have to royalty in America is the Kennedy family. I've always been appreciative of the late president's dedication to the performing arts. I never met President Kennedy, and never shook his son's hand. Still, many years later, it was a pleasure to visit the John F. Kennedy Center for the Performing Arts in the summer of 2012 when my wife Sherry was invited there to attend a seminar. She must have made a great impression, because in early 2014 she was invited back to lead a seminar on storytelling for children with special needs.

▲▲

On another expedition, this time while hiking Yellowstone National Park in Wyoming, I went deep into the forest on a solo wilderness hike. Customarily, we hiked in pairs or small groups, but this day I felt like experiencing America's first national park without the chatter of fellow hikers. I had hiked perhaps two miles into the Yellowstone Wilderness when something caught my eye. It happened very suddenly as I strode along the well-worn trail. I saw what I thought was a huge boulder in the middle of the trail ahead. The terrain nearby was not especially steep, so it seemed unlikely that a boulder would have rolled down an adjacent slope and come to rest in the middle of a maintained trail.

I stopped and considered how a rock the size of a mini-van

might have rolled onto the trail. There were no other boulders in view, and this one would have been large enough to weigh a ton.

I stood, continuing to study this "rock" from perhaps a distance of fifty paces. I noticed it was partially covered with a brown and black fungus, and that the fungus was on its east face. That was abnormal. In the northern hemisphere fungi usually grow on the north side of a rock or tree.

To study this anomaly better, I crept closer very cautiously. When I drew within twenty feet of the boulder, I observed that it seemed to be pulsating! Could it be a freshly deposited meteorite containing some form of extraterrestrial life?! Now in awe, I slowly tiptoed closer. Part of the "boulder" unfurled before me and the head of a bison bull reared up with a snort!

Aw man, I thought, *I'm twenty feet from a full-grown bison looking at me with fiery black eyes on the sides of his head, nostrils sniffing the air and checking me out.*

My attention went to the horns, those formidable horns, which could be charging me at any moment. The darker color of their tips caught my eye; was that dried blood from a season of dominance battles? I froze, letting him sniff the air. After what seemed like a life-time—*my lifetime*—I slunk slowly backward, doing the moonwalk, never losing eye contact with the big guy. I remembered the Three Stooges segment, "Niagara Falls!" "Slowly we turn, step by step, inch by inch ..."

When the bison decided I was not a threat, he lowered his massive head and returned to his snooze. Turning finally, I sought a different trail to explore. *Even my future Bond Girls,* I said to myself, *will be impressed with this story.* Beyond Bond, I wondered how martial-arts expert Bruce Lee would have handled an encounter with a full grown bull bison? Karate Master Masatatsu Oyama took off a bull's horn in a match! That answer was to come a few years later with a male swan!

On another park visit a year later, after listening to an evening ranger talk at Glacier National Park in northern Montana, I was headed back to the lodge. The resident park ranger had warned campers and visitors that the winds were very high and that everyone should be careful driving back across the mountain roads. When I reached Going to the Sun Road, a narrow and extremely high-altitude roadway that is only open seasonally, my car radio broke in with a weather bulletin. Fifty-mile-per-hour winds were blowing through the park. Shortly after that, while negotiating a hairpin turn on the mountainside, I seemed to lose steering control. The wind had picked my car up, off the roadway! Frantically, I tried to regain control by turning the steering wheel, but got no traction from the tires. Suddenly, the car slammed back down on the ground. My palms were sweating, my throat dry, and heart was racing as I prayed my way back to the lodge. Many nights later, I lay awake wondering, *What if the car had gone off the 1,000-foot cliff, which had no guard rails on the side?*

Going through my memories of the scenario repeatedly in my mind, I came to the same conclusion time after time. *I had achieved lift off!* Even without James Bond's fancy British Aston-Martin motorcar, I—the once and future First Black James Bond—*had driven into the air!*

CHAPTER TWENTY-EIGHT

Whoa—Big Boy!

UNLIKE MY BEING UNABLE to take mule rides into the Grand Canyon, my traveling expedition to Grand Teton National Park in Jackson Hole, Wyoming, offered a whole different experience. I saw a stable where tourists could rent a horse and take a trail ride along the lake. Unfortunately, our trail did not take us up the sheer eastern wall of Grand Teton Mountain, a 14,000-foot natural edifice on which America's Alpine team trains. For a modest price, I signed on to join several cowboys and trail bosses with an assorted group of tourists, all looking to take a leisurely ride around the lake there.

So it was with a carefree spirit that I mounted my steed as the trail bosses gave us a tutorial on riding. No 5,000 foot-deep canyon, no vertical mountainside; what could go wrong? Everything was fine until I cleared my throat. My horse whinnied loudly and bucked!

A trail boss asked, "What's going on over there, partner?"

"I only cleared my throat of some dust."

He rode over and looked at my horse and replied; "Oh, I see, you're riding Gunpowder."

I thought, *Oh this is good, I'm riding Gunpowder!* If I clear my throat on the ride, this animal may whip around, launch at full speed, and take off to the stables … with or without a rider in the saddle!"

Nothing was more frightening than feeling 1,500 pounds of pure muscle tense up under me during my very first horseback ride!

CHAPTER TWENTY-NINE
This "New Thing Called Storytelling"

IN THE SAME YEAR THAT I MET JACKIE TORRENCE (1988), another door opened for me as a performing storyteller. Sandy McDonnell, CEO of McDonnell Douglass Corporation, then a major aircraft manufacturer, got together with other CEOs and educators in St. Louis to create PREP, the Personal Responsibility Education Program. The idea was to help young people find answers to the many moral and ethical problems facing America in the 1980s. TV news was full of the Iran-Contra hearings and Ivan Boesky and his Wall Street raiders taking "crime off the streets and putting it into the suites." Mr. McDonnell wanted St. Louis school children to learn character education in the schools without educators being "preachy and dictatorial."

It was decided that children would respond best to a team cast led by a character similar to Big Bird and others on Sesame Street. Doug Kincaid, creator of baseball Cardinal's "Fred Bird," was selected to operate inside the costume of a four-foot tall "Grouchie Gator." I was to be his storytelling cohort and buddy on the Channel 4 TV set of *Gator Tales*—a cabin in a Louisiana swamp. The show revolved around Grouchie's learning curve about social concepts like teamwork and cooperation, honesty, respect, self-esteem, and honesty. We taped the show Thursday mornings ahead of the weekly broadcast. As Grouchie addressed the studio audience of kids, I would walk on camera making an exaggerated show of overhearing the situation.

I'd say "Grouchie, I was in the library the other day and found the perfect story to answer your problem!" Then I proceeded to tell a story that illustrated the appropriate character lesson for the show. I learned to sequence the story to include a cliffhanger before each of the two commercial breaks. Parents told me that kids watching at home on Saturday mornings figured out the solution during commercial breaks and were thrilled to hear their ideas confirmed when the story resumed. The show was widely popular in the Saint Louis market and the sponsors were delighted.

A series of questions was given to select schools in the PREP program to pass out the next school week as a review of the theme. The show was such a success that it won three regional Emmy Awards and was nominated for a fourth. *The Captain Kangaroo Special* on PBS was our only real competition during that golden era of "kid-vid," 1988-1994.

Some people eventually had issues with the whole "character education" concept in America, saying it was being usurped by conservative groups who espoused that their moral/ethical belief system was superior to the liberals. So it goes in the parallel universe of American politics.

In 1988, I was invited to come to the North Shore of Chicago, to Evanston, Illinois, to perform. It was my first time to perform as a storyteller outside of the Saint Louis area. On the bill were Lyn Rubright, Syd Lieberman, Jay O'Callahan, Jim May, and Jackie Torrence. Jackie's work was already legendary in 1988, and I was honored to be on the program with her and the other remarkable talents. Jackie, Syd, Jim and Jay had all previously appeared at the National Storytelling Festival, so I was awe-struck as I performed my first story, "Anansi the Spider and His Six Sons," in their presence. Lyn Rubright was also nationally-known in storytelling circles, so my anxiety was working overtime.

In my excitement prior to going on stage, I had applied too much talcum powder under my T-shirt. My intent was just to keep the sweating and nervousness at a minimum. During my set, when I made flamboyant gestures under the theatre lighting, puffs of talc would waft into the air. I did my best to ignore this unintended distraction and completed my story to general applause.

Later, Jim May and Jay O'Callahan said, "Wow, you make magic with your stories!" A bit embarrassed by what I saw as the distraction of flying talc, I explained that it was not the effect I was going for. Reflecting on the positive response to what had actually been a mistake, I paused to consider that the unintended effect had won accolades from storytellers whom I admired greatly. Their reaction had taught me I should accept praise not only for those planned, practiced effects in which I took understandable pride, but also those magical mistakes that "work." A Great Spirit loves the struggling performer, just as much as the lost lamb of the Bible story.

Later, that story became a signature piece of mine … sans the powder.

Jackie asked me to join her for a dinner meeting that night at the Orrington Hotel, where she was staying. A rotund woman with penetrating eyes and an infectious smile, she said that I reminded her of an uncle and grandpa who told stories. She asked if I wanted to meet her booking agent in Portland, Oregon, and her recording producer in Chicago.

"Well, um … yes, ma'am!" I stammered.

From an oversized handbag, she withdrew her traveling schedule. I was amazed as she showed me her calendar of gigs from coast to coast and internationally. Asking if I wanted to do this type of work, she smiled at me like a loving aunt, who wanted only the best for me. What, I wondered, had I done to deserve such generosity from one of the most successful professional storytellers in the world? Having watched me perform only once, this big-hearted woman was inviting me into the "big leagues" of her art. Much later in my mentorship, she told me that there are many people in the storytelling world, as in all professions, who are kind, warm, generous, selfless, giving, and joyful. Then, she cautioned me, there are those who are the exact opposite. After elaborating on this subject in great detail, she finished with, "Just keep focused on the good in people and persist in moving your career forward. Some will help you and others will thwart and sabotage your efforts to succeed at every turn." She spoke prophesy—from experience. I have met both kinds.

As Jackie and I concluded our initial meeting in Evanston, she ended by saying that we needed to continue to stay in touch. Shortly after that, her agent invited me to the Association of Performing Arts Presenters Conference the next year in New York City at the Hilton in Manhattan, where I landed my first $2,000 storytelling gig.

Jackie accompanied me to an appointment with her recording producer in Chicago. Jackie had previously made three sixty minute recordings (on cassette, which was the primary medium in those days) with the man, and now she was introducing me to him as a new talent. Within a year, I had visited his studio and recorded *Why Mosquitoes Buzz in People's Ears* and *Norfolk Tales*, my first storytelling products. When both audio cassettes won the Parents' Choice Gold Award, Jackie was as delighted as I was.

Jackie and I became friends and were always in touch. She would phone me when I was traveling, telling me about her work, her daughter, and granddaughter, and her home in Salisbury and Granite Quarry, North Carolina. She drove a Lincoln Town Car with the license plate declaring, "STORYLADY," and that she was. Her joy in my blossoming storytelling career was such a great reward, and her friendship was truly heartwarming. It was a special treat to be invited to perform in any storytelling festival where she was also on the bill. Her dynamic storytelling delivery were unmatched by anyone in the business when we met. She introduced me to Jimmy Neil Smith, founder of The National Storytelling Festival, and Lee Pennington of the Corn Island Festival.

Her health was another matter. Always a very ample woman, Jackie had a weight problem that seemed to be a clear and present danger. For me, it was reminiscent of watching my earlier fellow performing friends, Zack and Mack. Like them, Jackie was locked in an existential battle with obesity. In the end, it would claim her life, as it had Zack and Mack.

Jackie used her expressive face, her large eyes, and her hands, always neatly manicured and adorned with fine rings, to express every character and every emotion in ways that other storytellers could only admire. Jackie always requested a piano bench on stage. She spoke into a boom mic lowered to her mouth level. When she intoned her amazing range of voices, she worked magic with her face and hands. She demonstrated a sense of timing that was without equal. I found that event organizers, school systems, and others were calling my office and hiring me sight unseen, just on her recommendation. No storyteller ever had a better or more selfless friend.

In 2004, my wife Sherry and I were conducting a storytelling residency at the Hong Kong International School. One morning before our first session of the day, we stopped at a café for coffee. Making use of their free Internet service, we both checked our emails. The news that Jackie had fallen at her home in North Carolina, claimed by a heart attack, was the first thing we read. I was mortified, and so was Sherry. My day was spent trying not to re-live Jackie's anguish at being unable to get up from the floor, and at the pain she must have experienced lying there. Jackie was by herself at the time of her fall and heart attack. Nobody would ever know what pain she felt, what last thoughts occupied her as the darkness closed in, and the angels arrived to claim her.

Struggling to go on with my work day, I directed my mind to my "happy place." The memory of a failed gig in New York City drew me in. Jackie and I had been invited to the city for an all-expense-paid conference that paid very well. Upon arrival in our four-star hotel, we were told that the organizers had canceled our work. They would pay us nothing. It was up to us to pay our air travel, our hotel expenses, ground transportation and food. Being in NYC, these expenses were not insignificant. The loss of income was a shock to both of us. Jackie called our agent, who wired the money for us to stay until we could re-book our flights.

Although we were disappointed in the trip, I sought solace at the piano bar that evening. As I sat, staring blankly out over the harbor, the singer on piano ended her set with Billy Joel's "New York State of Mind." In an instant, the trip was complete and fulfilled. The disappointment of not performing left me. I was embraced by the magic of the city once again.

CHAPTER THIRTY

I Don't Know If I Hit Forty or Forty Hit Me

PART OF MY SO-CALLED MID-LIFE CRISIS was the urge to buy a brand new, fire-engine-red Honda Prelude with a spoiler on the trunk. I sported the racy car around town, letting anyone who asked drive it, while I sat nervously in the passenger seat hoping their foot would not be too heavy. Everyone who sat behind the wheel wanted to get it on the highway and "turn the horses loose." Well, the Lord giveth and the Lord taketh away.

One weekend I was working in Kansas City. When I took my bags to the car that Saturday morning, I saw that the spoiler had been ripped from the trunk! *Someone needed it more than me,* I thought. Insurance replaced it.

A month later, in early January, I went to Atlanta. On the nine-hour drive back to St. Louis, I drove into a blinding blizzard. Snow was coming down sideways and the temperature was in the teens. Four hours from St. Louis, the Prelude started overheating. Steam started pouring out of the hood and vents. Suddenly the heater stopped working and ice started forming on the inside of the windshield. Summoning all of my angels, I scraped ice from the window and tried frantically to find an exit with a service station. Braced against the snow, I popped the hood. Carefully, I covered the radiator cap and turned cautiously. A whoosh of steam came from the car and crystal-lized in midair. It was like my own personal Old Faithful right there in the blizzard. I purchased two cans of anti-freeze and poured them into the radiator. After a total of four cans of anti-freeze, I pointed that red car back onto the interstate, where traffic was crawling at forty miles per hour due to blowing snow. Lane markings were invisible because of deep snow. Every car had its emergency flashers on as it inched forward.

Two hours later the heater stopped working, the windshield iced on the inside again, and smoke or steam billowed out of the engine compartment again. Again, I found an exit with a service station. Again, I tipped up first two—then two more—cans of anti-freeze into the radiator. Again, I re-joined the interstate traffic in the blizzard. An eternity later, I parked the car at home in St. Louis, just when the steam poured out again. Exhausted and prayerful in thanks for arriving home safely, I went to bed and slept soundly, dreaming of emergency flashers as far as the eye can see in a blizzard.

The next morning, the snow was eight inches deep on the ground and the red Prelude was covered completely. At mid-day when the streets were cleared, I called AAA to come service my car. I went out to clean it off when the truck came. I got inside and tried the engine. Nothing happened. No lights, no engine noise, nothing.

When the mechanic arrived, he asked me to pop the hood while I sat in the car. He pulled up the hood and yelped, "Oh my goodness, sir. Come look at this!" I got out and went to look. He said the manifold, the top of the engine housing, and the spark plugs had melted on top of the engine. "How did you drive this car like this?" This engine melted from the heat; it is totaled!" The car was not drivable, so he hoisted it on the tow and we went to the station. I called the insurance company and they sent out an adjuster who confirmed the car was totaled and had to be replaced. With the purchase of a conventional blue Civic, my life toned down considerably.

CHAPTER THIRTY-ONE

The Aurora Borealis at 35,000 Feet

ONCE, WHILE RETURNING from a performance tour in Alaskan schools and libraries, I was on a red-eye flight from Anchorage to Seattle. I was thinking of my disappointment at not having seen the Northern Lights while so close to the North Pole. During my visit, it had been January—perfect weather for observing the glorious natural illumination of the skies. Our plane had departed the Anchorage airport at 1 a.m. for the flight to Seattle. It was one of those flights called a "red eye" because that's what condition your eyes are in after trying to stay awake for the middle-of-the-night flight. As we arrived at our cruising altitude of 35,000 feet, I happened to glance out of my window. My head did a double take. Outside my window, the midnight sky was aflame with swirling colors of eerie light. *There they were*, the Aurora Borealis. Floating through the upper atmosphere was an array of green and red lights, undulating between the stars.

I was taken with the realization that the Aurora Borealis is formed by a combination of ice crystals in the upper atmosphere, sunspots, and electro-magnetic pulses from the Arctic Circle. I sat with my face pressed to the window, transfixed by a private view of an awesome phenomenon, from an airplane with a controlled environment. Watching the colors change, I thought, *How fitting that Phillip Pullman's* His Dark Materials *uses the Northern Lights as a way to enter other dimensions.*

I love to fly with a legal pad and pen, to be prepared when the flow of images comes like an opened floodgate. It is my practice to request a window seat since I always want to look at the terrain and the horizon. Some of my deeper thoughts, more memorable images, and most serene realizations come while in flight.

After performing in Cardiff, Wales, and Northern Ireland, we returned to London on an international flight, following a most indirect route back to the States. We took off from London's Gatwick Airport, heading north over northern Europe at 35,000 feet. The pilot said our flight plan would take us over Greenland, after which we would turn south and cross over Canada into U.S. airspace. He said we would then cross the Great Lakes on our path into Chicago O'Hare Airport.

When we crossed over Greenland, I looked out my window into the bright sunshine to the ocean below. There, five miles below, I watched thousands of icebergs that had broken off the glaciers. These masses of ice were clearly visible, floating in the Labrador Sea. I was amazed at how big they must be to be so clearly visible from such a great height. Like polka dots of random sizes, they speckled the sea below.

I could not help speculating about those icebergs, about how rapidly they were calving from the edges of glaciers where their formation had taken thousands if not millions of years. How quickly must our climate be changing to propel such acceleration of their departure from the mother glacier? While I saw them as a beautiful phenomenon, their sheer numbers seemed also to be a cautionary sign. Rapid changes can be fraught with danger in any process, and rapid climatological change seemed to portend greater potential danger than anything else on my personal radar screen. What might lay ahead at the intersection of beauty and danger?

My travels as a storyteller took me to several continents within the last several years. Everywhere I went, people worried aloud about changes in temperatures, storm patterns, sea levels, and habitats for species on which humans depend, not to mention other species we hold in awe. Many, many years ago Rachel Carson wrote *A Silent Spring* in which she warned us of not protecting the environment. We did not listen carefully enough.

From my home in St. Louis, Missouri, my travels have taken me to Florida by way of New York City, to Alaska and on to London. From there, storytelling gigs drew me to Ireland, Wales, and then all the way to Hong Kong. I returned via Hawaii and San Francisco, then north to Seattle and back home. Other storytelling work has drawn me on to Singapore, Indonesia, Bangkok, Thailand, Manila in the Philippines, and Austria. My eyes have been opened to climate change of many types through personal observation. Everywhere I have been, observant hosts have also shared their concerns about what is happening to this irreplaceable place we call Earth. People who have hosted me for performances in their diverse cities have said, as if with one voice, "This is the strangest weather we have ever seen."

"This is the warmest weather I can remember."

"This is the mildest/coldest/shortest/longest winter we have ever had."

"The frequency/severity of storms—hail storms, tornados, and hurricanes—surprise and frighten my family."

"What happened to predictable seasons?"

"Drought like this is killing our crops and emptying our lakes."

Gone are the days when my idea of weather prediction was to look at the clouds, sense the humidity level on my skin, and check the wind by wetting a finger and thrusting it into the air. That country bumpkin who once felt knowledgeable and confident in the regularity of climate is no longer confident or at ease as he moves about the planet. I feel more sophisticated about climate these days, but much less confident or at ease. Extreme weather patterns on a global scale are now a fact of life. I am personally experiencing global weather changes that range in the extreme.

Plastics in the oceans are choking the sea life to death and wreaking havoc on the currents. Fishes and mammals are losing their bearings and ending up in areas not natural to their habitat. Birds are flying to unknown areas seeking food no longer available in their original habitat. Millions of honey bees are missing in action from their pollinating duties.

The Deep Water Horizon oil spill has caused horrific harm to the Gulf of Mexico. Even President Barack Obama was prompted to lament, "All we can do is pray things will be okay down there." There will come a time when we finally wake up and stop using the nineteenth century technology of oil and coal to power the world.

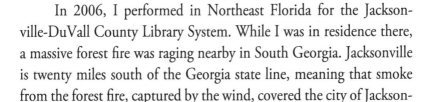

In 2006, I performed in Northeast Florida for the Jacksonville-DuVall County Library System. While I was in residence there, a massive forest fire was raging nearby in South Georgia. Jacksonville is twenty miles south of the Georgia state line, meaning that smoke from the forest fire, captured by the wind, covered the city of Jacksonville and most of northeastern Florida.

Looking up at the gray smoke, I seemed to be watching clouds of airborne charcoal. Soot fell throughout the city, on sidewalks, steps, railings, windshields, and park benches. Upon standing after a respite, I had to sweep the back of my trousers to remove tree char that had floated in from Georgia and deposited itself where I had been sitting.

After completing my responsibilities in Jacksonville, I was driven to the Jacksonville Airport to await the tedium that is the homebound trip after exciting work. On that day, the tedium would not last long. As my plane rose on the first leg of my return flight to St. Louis, making its ascent from Jacksonville Airport, there was a sudden lurch followed by the steepest, deepest dive I have ever experienced as a seasoned business traveler. Everyone around me gasped and grabbed the arms of their seats. Just as we were about to relax after the plane righted itself and resumed its ascent—before we could recover—the plane went into another steep and deep dive. Another round of urgent gasps and moans passed through the passenger cabin.

After we eventually leveled off at our cruising altitude, the intercom came to life with the pilot's voice.

"Sorry ladies and gentlemen, we had to take that drastic evasive maneuver. We were headed into the belly of another plane before we saw it on our radar screen. We were making our ascent blindly in the smoke." I turned to the sympathetic eyes of the woman across the aisle, and together we raised our hands in the universal gesture of prayer. Having experienced a near-death moment together, we were bound together in gratitude and relief. I was to experience many other encounters where metaphysical or spiritual entities would intervene to assure me of protection by a surrounding "force." At these times, I felt an affirming feeling that my purpose for being was not yet realized.

CHAPTER THIRTY-TWO
Critter Encounters

WHILE TAKING A NIGHT CLASS at UMSL to finish my degree program, a classmate asked if I wanted a puppy. My friend said her husky/

shepherd mix had delivered six pups, and at six weeks they needed a new home. One day after an evening class, I went to visit the family of my classmate and her extended family of puppy dogs. When I arrived at the house, my classmate's husband and daughter greeted me at the door. Emerging from the kitchen, my friend asked, "You were serious; you want a puppy?"

I knew I did, but my new job as a traveling storyteller plus the fact that I was then living alone combined to make pet ownership a problem. While mulling all of this over, I noticed one pup who was away from the litter, watching a parakeet in a cage on the coffee table. The pup had the most curious look on her face wondering what kind of animal the parakeet was. "How cute," I thought.

The little female cutie went home with me that night. Despite my heart going out to her, I knew within a few days that I could not keep a dog in my apartment since my constant travel would be an issue. Reluctantly I gave the pup over to my agent, Jan Dolan, who *thought* she was the new owner. In my mind, that dog was now a foster dog with me having visiting rights! HAH! I found out when the pup matured that I was dealing with an alpha female loner, a huntress! Every chance I got while not performing, I would take Justine out to Forest Park, a large and beautiful area in Central Saint Louis so we could "play!" Following are some experiences of a boy and his dog.

While walking the husky/shepherd mix on a leash, I noticed she loved to sniff inside bushes and hedges. I thought she was just curious, sniffing territory marked by other dogs. Little did I know this huntress was seeking prey the whole time. I figured it out when one morning on our walking/sniffing jaunt she suddenly sticks her entire head into a hedge and the entire bush starts to shake, rattle, and roll! She suddenly drew her head back and there was a cat wrapped around her face! I freaked! I know the cat was freaking out, too. The only one in control of the situation was the dog—a calculating predator had snagged her catch! In a near panic, I jerked the leash backward and yelled "NO!" The cat popped out of her mouth and ran like it was scalded across the street, hopped a fence and disappeared! I thought, *I can't believe this.* Justine had a different look, *I can't believe it got away!*

In another incident, I was walking the alpha-female-huntress-husky-shepherd on a leash when she spotted a man coming around the corner with his wirehaired terrier. I immediately wrapped the leather leash around my wrist when I saw her hackles rise up on the back of her neck. The guy was aware of the aggression Justine was showing and veered away from us. Justine reared up on her hind legs, barking and snarling. Just when I pulled back on the leash … it snapped in two! Yes! Snapped in two. Justine liked to chew on it in her periods of boredom.

She suddenly lurched forward and attacked! Rushing the terrier, she engaged the other dog in a tangle of fur and snapping canine teeth. The terrier was having none of this "Queen of the Road" stuff. I must say, the man must have thought I made Justine attack his dog because he couldn't see the broken leash in my hand. In his shock I had the presence of mind to rush into the fray of battling pooches and grab Justine by her haunches and pull as hard as I could! When I extricated her from the fight, I noticed the man had never let go of his dog's leash. I wrapped what was left of Justine's leash around her miserable neck, begging forgiveness from the guy all the while. Justine and I hustled away from the scene with much dispatch! As we walked, she had that show dog gait in her step and panted heavily with a look of proud superiority on her face.

What self-respecting dog doesn't like to chase squirrels? Justine had a zero tolerance for them (or any other creature that challenged her alpha-female position, for that matter). One day I was walking with Justine and two nephews of Jan Dolan, Connor and Jason. We walked to a large churchyard where there were a few trees and lots of lawn area to romp. Removing her leash, I joined the boys in watching her sniff and mark her territory. A squirrel didn't like Justine being under the grove of trees. He began chirping loudly in his squirrel voice, sucking air through his big front teeth. Justine looked up and began barking back at the squirrel. The squirrel didn't like being scolded by a dog and started hopping from branch to branch, limb to limb, flipping its bushy tail violently up and down. Justine ran from the trunk of one tree to the other putting both front paws on the trees and barking wildly.

The boys and I were being entertained and I thought how cute it all was, until the squirrel made a rookie mistake in its routine. It missed the branch it was aiming for and fell to the ground, about three feet from Justine. Time stood still. None of us, me, the boys, the dog, or the squirrel, could believe what had just occurred. Justine and the now compromised tree rodent stared at one another for a brief moment. Suddenly, the squirrel dashed for a clump of hedges with Justine in hot pursuit. After a moment of the bushes shaking and thrashing, Justine came back out … without the squirrel in her mouth. We all got out of there without knowing the fate of the clumsy critter that almost fell into the mouth of a predator. It reminded me so much of the silly squirrels who, in such a panic to run to the safety of their own tree, will run in front of a moving car thinking they can make it. Well, sometimes they do, and sometimes not.

I seem to have the strangest encounters with dogs. This one occurred a few years earlier, when I was in college. Jogging one night, I saw a man walking in the opposite direction and I paid no notice to him except to run on the right of him. After a moment passed I saw that he was walking two full-grown Dobermans *off-leash!* They both saw me at the same time as they were stalking and sniffing in front of him. When they and I made eye contact, I came to a screeching halt! They bared their canine teeth and I saw those menacing eyes fixed on me as if to say "there is the rabbit!" I broke into a karate stance as they charged. I yelled, "Key-aiiii!" They stopped, turned, and ran in the opposite direction whimpering past their master. He turned, looked at his killer dogs running back home, and then turned back again to look at me with astonishment. I gave him the short arms look (both elbows at my sides, forearms out and palms up, head cocked to one side). He jogged after his hounds as I walked home slowly, wondering if they had seen some invisible force behind me that frightened them. That remains a mystery to this day.

Even though I claimed Justine as *my dog,* I cannot say the same for the next doofus animal that my agent, Jan Dolan, chose all by herself. Henry was definitely *her* dog.

Henry, the 110-pound, three-foot tall shepherd and border collie mix can be very easily startled sometimes. One day after taking a break from my office in the addition to Jan's house, I went to make a cup of tea in the kitchen. She was loading her dishwasher at the time. Well, at one point, Jan turned to the sink to wash the rim out of a plate as Henry comes ambling into the kitchen. He saw the door down on the now fully loaded dishwasher and proceeded to lick some food stains off a plate. When he tried to lift his head up, his collar got caught on a part of the dish rack. He pulled harder and harder, but the collar was firmly caught in the rack. He panicked, yelping and howling. Then he pulled the entire rack out of the dishwasher, sending dishes and silverware flying all over the kitchen floor!

The more noise and crashing he heard, the more Henry freaked out. Eyeing the dog door across the kitchen, he dashed for it, yelping and scattering dishes and cutlery. His massive frame disappeared through the dog door into the backyard. Not engineered for such a contingency, his collar ripped free from his neck. Henry escaped the mayhem he had caused. Jan and I watched the whole thing and stood silently amid the aftermath of a kitchen disaster of monumental proportions. Some dishes actually survived Henry's purge, but most did not. Jan was physically shaken and I was thoroughly entertained! Now, that's a sight one doesn't see every day.

CHAPTER THIRTY-THREE
The Vizsla and The Doggie Slobber

MY MOTHER-IN-LAW, Nettie Austin, had a dog with the breed name, Vizsla. She named the dog Nageé. He had a mind of his own, which seems the nature of these animals. He would be bold enough to come sneakily behind people while they were at dinner and grab a food item, it mattered not what, off their plate. He would dash to the living room and eat it straight away. I know for a fact he would eat whatever was available. One morning at breakfast, that dog grabbed a half-peeled banana from my place setting and hauled it off into the living room to devour it. It was his ill-gotten booty, as pirates would say. Little did he know I would be in hot pursuit within three seconds! I caught him in the act of eating my half-peeled banana and rushed toward him. Startled, he ran from room to room, with me in pursuit, shouting, "Give me back my banana, you mutt!"

After three loops through the house, Nageé decided to just gulp down the food and not give me a chance to extract it from his thieving jaws. To my amazement, he ate the peel and all! Afterward, he gave me that "top of the pecking order" look. *I win, you lose! I get the food, you get to brood!* All this time, Sherry and Nettie were at the breakfast table cracking up. A circus had broken out with Nageé running from the kitchen, down the hall, through the living room, eating on the half-peeled banana while watching for me, to see if I was still in pursuit.

We retired to the living room after breakfast, Nettie and Sherry still giggling over the circus act. Nageé was still sniffing at all our laps seeing what was in our drinking cups. I decided, "It's Not Over!" I placed my teacup down and pounced on him suddenly, with the speed of a Ninja. Grabbing his opposite legs, I yanked him on his side. Immediately, I jumped him, pinning him to the floor. As he struggled to break free, I laid more weight on him as in a wrestling match. The only thing I allowed to move on this hound was his head. I was going to prove to him once and for all I'm the alpha, he's the beta. Sherry and Nettie were impressed at this deft move to put Nageé under restraint. He looked up at me with big winsome eyes, and laid his head back down. Suddenly, he looked up at me and sneezed right in my face! Doggie slobber covered my entire face! I reeled back and started pulling my T-shirt up to wipe the phlegm from my face and eyes. Nageé, in the meantime, jumped to his feet and did a little victory bark. As I heard the raucous laughter of Nettie and Sherry, I sat back down to finish wiping my face. Oh, ladies and gentlemen, *It's not over!*

Nageé came over to me on the couch and proceeded to wipe the drool from his snout on my pants. I was frozen thinking, *Is he actually wiping drool on my pants*, when Sherry yelled out, "He's wiping drool on your pants. HA HA HA HA!" He then went to another room doing his Top Dog strut, as Sherry and Nettie "howled" with laughter!

All my life I have loved dogs and cats equally. Dogs are lovable for their companionship and funny, playful nature. Cats are mysterious and reclusive … until they want total attention from the person who is "living with them." They are agile, quick, and powerful for such a small animal, just like the Kung Fu Masters I grew to idolize. I have learned much by watching how these two animals act in their environment and interact with humans.

CHAPTER THIRTY-FOUR

Tension in the Foyer

IN MARCH 1995, I was invited to go to Oakland, California, to perform in a video called "Basic Training for Boys." It was to be a humorous but instructive look at teaching boys how to clean the house, do chores without being told, to wash, iron, fold, and put their clothes away. Imagine that! Well, after the filming was "wrapped," my friend insisted on driving me on a tour of San Francisco, Oakland, and Berkley, California—together known as the Bay Area. Who was I to refuse such an offer?

When we arrived in Berkley, we went to an espresso bar called Au Coquelet Café on University Avenue for a cup of java. My favorite espresso bar order was a soy latté introduced to me by professional storyteller and actress, Brenda Wong Aoki, when we were working in Vancouver British, Columbia. Ironically, Brenda is from San Francisco. When we were at a gig together in Vancouver, she asked me if I wanted to go get a cappuccino or latté on our break. I said, "A what?

A who?" She looked at me and said, "Come, my son, into the world of gourmet coffee." Fast-forward back to the scene of my Bay Area tour. When my friend and I reached the espresso shop, he said I should get out and find a table while he parked. I complied and entered the café through a door with a small, enclosed foyer.

A tall man was talking to a woman in the foyer, requiring me to squeeze past them to reach the main door. Turning my torso sideways as I deftly moved past them, making sure not to brush against them, I felt a "disturbance in the Force." An intense uneasiness came over me, as if the man was staring at me. An innate defense mechanism kicked into gear at the back of my brain. Must I defend myself? Momentum carried me to and through the main door, and the feeling subsided. I was escorted to a table and sat. My buddy came in shortly afterward, through the then-clear foyer. The couple had moved on. We gave our order and settled in. When the java arrived, my buddy said, "Bobby, right behind you at a table reading a book and having an espresso is Eldridge Cleaver."

I asked, "Former minister of information of the Black Panther Party in the '60s and '70s?"

"Yes!"

I turned around and saw the man whom I felt the visual daggers from in the foyer. Even with my back turned to him, I felt his presence. Eldridge Cleaver sat there, a tall African-American man with a goatee, leather jacket and shades, now in his early 60's, reading a book. This is the same man whose record *DIG!* was snatched off the turntable twenty-six years earlier at my community college in St. Louis, igniting the events I experienced as a freshman.

A major force during the social upheaval of the 1960s, the Black Panther Party for Self Defense was an internationally-known black militant organization. Cleaver was one of their Keynote Speakers and a member of the Central Committee, the core leadership of the organization. Also in leadership were Huey P. Newton and Bobby Seale. In my sophomore year in college, Eldridge Cleaver's book, *Soul on Ice,* was required reading in English Literature.

When J. Edgar Hoover and his FBI declared war on the Black Panther Party, the organization was dismantled and its leaders suffered a variety of ill fates. Many were killed by assassins, in police shootouts, or found themselves imprisoned on any charge a local, state or federal prosecutor could make stick. Others, like Cleaver, sought voluntary exile overseas. Cleaver went to Algiers, Algeria. When the political climate changed in America in the 1980s and Ronald Reagan became president, Cleaver became a conservative Republican. Cleaver even created a line of provocative men's apparel with a genitalia pouch on the outside of the pants. For some reason, it never caught on.

Here was a man I had admired greatly in my youth, a man whose courage literally changed the world, and he was seated five feet away. Memories of his exploits and close encounters with the United States government went through my mind. As I sat, I surreptitiously turned my chair around to glance at the man whose aura filled that space we inhabited together. I sipped on an eight-ounce soy latté and considered how lives enter our world and then slip slowly away.

CHAPTER THIRTY-FIVE

Discoveries on a Not-So-Dark Continent

IN THE SUMMER OF **1993,** I was thrilled to be invited to go to Ghana in West Africa and Cairo, Egypt. The man who invited me to perform in Egypt was Akbar Muhammad, a St. Louis businessman and human rights activist. This was my first international trip and I was more than excited. Six weeks prior to departure, I submitted to the customary disease shots one gets when going into a Third-World country. Although I abhor needles, the pretravel excitement fueled the courage a scaredy cat like me required to keep the doctor's appointment. With my left arm recovered from the shots and my shiny new passport in hand, I boarded a flight from St. Louis to Chicago, followed by the epic flight from Chicago O'Hare to Cairo, Egypt.

On our first stop in Cairo, I was overwhelmed to be in such a foreign environment. After we had taxied to our gate, the Egypt Air jumbo jet shut its engines down and the familiar ding sounded for us to get up and deplane. Walking across the tarmac, I felt like Neil Armstrong stepping onto the moon. It was a momentous milestone in my life; I was on foreign soil on the other side of the world. What a rush that was!

Walking into the main terminal after going through customs, I was shocked by the presence of military personnel eyeing arriving passengers at every point throughout the terminal. These were not ordinary military policemen; they were decked out in full battle gear and carried AK-47 automatic weapons. While I was shocked to see the military presence so dominant, my lasting impression of Cairo was of the charming culture and first-class accommodations we enjoyed there.

This was eight years before Sept. 11, 2001, and twenty years before the Arab Spring of 2013. While the military presence was definitely something new, I still didn't have the feeling of being on foreign soil until we stepped outside. The brown landscape, the stark white architecture, and the Mediterranean humidity served immediate notice that I was not in Illinois any longer. Like Dorothy dropped down into Oz, I knew I was a stranger in a strange land. Suddenly, the reality that my incredibly long flight had deposited me in a totally different culture and a shockingly different climate was abundantly clear.

I checked into our hotel, which was ultra-modern, with en-suite baths and air conditioning. But we were instructed to drink bottled water. Fortunately, it was provided in every room. Even though Egypt is considered a Third-World country, the ancient wisdom and knowledge of these people who built an advanced civilization millennia before the European nations is undeniable. The antiquities of the museums and the monuments stand as proof positive of the sophistication of Egypt centuries before our current calendar began. Since then, frequent wars of conquest by raiding European armies have slowed Egypt's progress.

If the hotel was starkly modern, the tour bus took me back a generation or two. Imagine a twenty-five-year-old American grade school bus, painted white inside and out, with a tour guide making announcements from a standing position beside the driver. The interior was steamy hot when we boarded, but the guide smiled and assured us that the air conditioning would be turned on when we left the hotel. What he called air conditioning was more like a roof-mounted fan. However, as the driver swung out into Cairo traffic, we were grateful for the fan. Cairo traffic was like a moving museum of every model of automobile manufactured in the Western world since JFK was president, with a hundred thousand motorbikes weaving in and out.

Our tour guide confirmed our expectation that our first stop was to be the Great Pyramid on the Giza Plateau. In school, I had read about this structure, and on American television I had seen documentaries about the anthropological digs that revealed its treasures. Also, I had seen countless movies and photos in which the magnificent structure played a supporting, if not central role. Soon I would walk up to its base. We were not scheduled to tour the inner chambers of the Great Pyramid because of on-going renovation work, but we were permitted to walk around it, as well as the Sphinx. I made certain that I had a window seat on the tour bus.

When we finally arrived on the Giza Plateau, there, looming outside of my window, were the Great Pyramid of Khufu (Cheops) and the two lesser pyramids. After our bus was parked, I pulled my camera from my backpack and joined the group outside. We proceeded to walk in the shadow of the pyramid, snapping pictures of the worn facia stones of the pyramid with its lesser sisters in the background. Of course, we happily exchanged cameras to snap photos of each other.

Also on the tour were Bob Law, legendary New York City talk radio host, and Jawanza Kunjufu, author of the then-popular book, *Countering the Conspiracy to Destroy Black Boys* (1985). I gained life experiences from them and they were just as entertained by my work onstage. There were thirty-five of us on the two-week bus tour. I was the only performing artist. The organizer asked me to perform twice and offered to reduce the cost of the trip by half. Instead of paying $3,000, I paid $1,500. It was a deal I could not pass up.

When we landed in Accra, Ghana, in West Africa, the terrain, the people, and the architecture were in sharp contrast to Cairo. Ghana is lush and green, sitting on the coast of the Gulf of Guinea. The Giza plateau was a high desert, but the capital city of Accra was resplendent in its verdant terrain. Ghana could not be confused with Kenya or Tanzania. We saw no elephants, zebras, or lions. The purpose of this stop was to spend most of our scheduled time visiting historical and cultural sites and towns in Ghana.

When we arrived at our village, each single guest was assigned a one- or two-room thatched dwelling and groups of two couples were assigned to thatched huts having three rooms. My one-room hut was a circular space fourteen feet across. The door consisted of a heavy drape of burlap cloth. Inside, along the walls were a worn three-drawer dresser, a single bed with a four-inch foam mattress, a mirror about two feet square, and a small table with two simple wooden chairs. To my surprise and delight, my hut also had a bathroom with running water and a working toilet.

The people in the countryside of Accra were as "citified" and urban as were those we met in Cairo, and they were incredibly friendly. Everyone met us with a huge smile and obvious curiosity about our lives in America. Ghanaians—at least in the villages we visited—travel rarely, mainly to acquire food or to visit relatives in nearby villages. The idea of a country whose population travels routinely for work and play clearly intrigued all but the best-educated of them.

Believing in education, as I do, I was curious to see the village schoolhouse and to meet the teaching staff. The local guides introduced me to two teachers, both native Ghanaians educated in the local universities. The teachers, one male and one female, were more than happy to take me to their four-room schoolhouse. I thought my hut was Spartan! Minister Akbar, the tour leader, wanted to show off this land where he split time between Ghana and St. Louis, Missouri. He showed us the best that Accra had to offer. Wherever we went, we were in comfortable surroundings and ate quality food.

I have to admit that I had a secret agenda for a personal style experiment while I was in Africa. Having many American friends whose hairstyle was more expressive of our African origins than my own modified Afro, I wanted to have extender braids put in my hair. I wanted twelve-inch braids.

When we walked to the village marketplace, I arranged to have my hair lengthened. The African stylists used horsehair braids, similar to those used on my djembe drummer back in St. Louis. I had often admired the style of Baba Kenya Ajanaku, who performed percussion for me on my spoken word poetry pieces. Kenya formerly toured with the famed Kathrine Dunham Troupe and Mor Thiam of Senegal. Thiam also worked with the Black Artists Group (BAG) in Saint Louis, where I performed poetry. Two Ghanaian women who spoke perfect English worked on my hair for four hours, one sitting on each side of me as I sat cross-legged in a large wooden chair with a cushion in their market stall. They burned the tips of dyed horsehair with candles and painstakingly braided each three-strand extension onto a few strands of my real hair. It was a grueling painstaking ordeal that I was determined to endure. *My goodness the patience and discipline!* Thinking of women around the world having to do this routinely, I was humbled.

When they were finished, I stood up and admired their handi-work in the mirror. A bit startled, but satisfied, I withdrew my wallet as their eyes doubled in size. I bowed first to one and then to the other, raised my hands in the universal sign of prayer, and thanked them. Paying them the equivalent of three hours' minimum wage salary in my country, I was delighted to see their eyes grow even larger. Later, a guide told me that what I had paid would be the equivalent of three days' hard labor pay in their households.

Looking at my reflection in the hut mirror that evening, I focused on a man I did not recognize. Oh, his eyes were familiar, and his ears were still there, but something about him was foreign to me. Over several hours, I found myself returning to the mirror to study *that man*. His heritage was mine—he was somewhat familiar— but somehow his possibilities were very different than the man from yesterday's mirror.

The unnatural feel of the additional hair—just the weight of it—was another aspect of the change it made in me. While the image was at least partially authentic, the bulk now attached to my head was unlike a hat or cap. It was not something I could take off to cool myself, or set aside to take a nap. To remove it would require four hours of two professionals working on me.

That night I thought I would go insane. The more I moved on the pillow, the more I heard this crunching and felt the scratchiness of my new hair. Finally, about three a.m., I went to the bathroom to stare at the braids in the mirror. I tugged on one or two to see if it would come loose. No chance of that, I sat on a chair in the dining area, willing myself into a deep meditation. *Stop the claustrophobia* was my focus. Living inside all that extra hair was threatening to drive me into an anxiety attack. I took an aspirin and sat some more in the dark room. Sleep came later when peace was restored in my core. The next morning, I was more adjusted to the change. Everyone in the group loved the change to my appearance.

Our bus tour operator had to scratch the nearby border country of Togo, just east of Ghana, from our schedule. A civil war was brewing there, and the tour company was wary of danger to our group and their bus. None of us cared at all that there was an omission from the tour.

The change in schedule meant that we would spend more time at the infamous slave castles on the coast. Those stone monuments may have looked like castles to Europeans, but not to African-Americans. We knew there were slave dungeons below ground level.

We all became silent as the tour guide took us down into the dungeons, down the cold, sweaty stone steps bellied by thousands of feet. When Africans were captured, our guide explained, the military captors had their pick of native women to take to their quarters. Everyone else was dragged into the cold, dark dungeons. In those cavernous cells, natives were "broken" for total obedience to the slave masters.

Standing in centuries of the blood, sweat, and tears of kidnapped people, we felt a twinge of the abject fear they surely felt, knowing they were being prepared for the trip across the Atlantic, a trip into lifelong slavery and a lifetime sentence of hard labor. It would be a voyage that fewer than seventy percent of them would survive.

The curator stepped to two huge wooden doors after his presentation. As those massive doors creaked on their ancient hinges, he said, "I will now open The Doors of No Return." We looked at one another, incredulous that anything else he could show us would exceed the degradation and horror of the chambers we had just seen.

When he opened the doors, what we saw was the Atlantic Ocean, now seen for the first time as a highway of brutality, hardship, and death. Beaches, wind-driven white clouds, and the endless blue of the ocean, all spoke in silent testimony to what enslaved Africans were to experience after leaving that place. In that moment, I envisioned hundreds of transatlantic ships moored in the distance, waiting for their cargo.

The following day, our guide took us inland to visit Ghanaians living in smoothly paved settlements relatively untouched by colonization and Western culture. Entering the village of the Ashanti, we experienced royalty, which was a great honor. It was an *al fresco* courtyard with lush plants and peacocks strutting about foraging. In both visits, the kings came out of their palaces in traditional dress and spoke a few moments welcoming us to their country and village. In a Q&A session with government officials in the town of Kumasi, I (as the only performing artist in the group) asked, "What is the importance of Anansi the Spider in your culture?"

A council woman broke into a big smile and exclaimed, "Anansi, him Spider! Every day when I was young, at 4:30 we would stop and have Anansi Time with the storyteller." In traditional West African storytelling, Anansi is a trickster who teaches us proper behavior through his negative example. In the psychology of Carl Jung, The Trickster is the "archetype" of our psyche that compels humans to get the best of or beguile others.

The next day brought one of the most memorable events of the entire trip. We arrived at the home of W.E.B. Dubois, the African-American author and social activist whose books are considered classics of American literature. I knew that he had passed away in 1963. I knew that he was one of the most important people in The Harlem Renaissance movement and in the entire Civil Rights movement in the USA. And I knew that Dubois was instrumental in founding the National Association for the Advancement of Colored People (NAACP). What I did not know, as we stepped off the bus, was that the visiting scholar who would present the story of W.E.B. DuBois was a woman I admired even more than the great man himself.

The visiting scholar and guest speaker that day at his home was Dr. Maya Angelou. Awestruck, we gathered in the front yard, sitting in chairs or standing, and listened as the exotic birds called from the nearby trees. Maya Angelou spoke for about forty-five minutes. She talked about DuBois as a historical figure, a man of ideas and a man of destiny. She spoke about his life in America and his life in Africa. She told us about the home site we were visiting, where DuBois lived last and where he died, too ill to make the trip to the 1963 March for Jobs and Freedom on Washington.

After her remarks, we toured the house, viewing his mementos, books, and his writing desk. As we did, I passed right by Ms. Angelou twice, but got so tongue-tied, all I could do was gawk and smile. The fact that I could not formulate words to address a person I admired so devotedly bugs me even today. I blame it on the braids. Yeah, it was the braids.

Returning to Chicago after the epic flight from Cairo, our group lined up at the airport screening area for U.S. Customs. When my turn came and I was beckoned up to one of the little cubicles, the agent inside said, "Welcome back to the Unites States." After the close-up history lesson and Spartan living we had just experienced, his words did have a great sound to them. In the back of my mind, a list of ordinary First World conveniences played happily in Technicolor. Still, after having seen and heard all that we had in Africa, conveniences took a back seat to human dignity in my thoughts. Was I relieved to be back in the USA? You bet. Was I grateful for all of its history? Not so much. The slave castles and "The Door of No Return" were in my thoughts.

I sported the braids for ten days, showing them off to approving friends, bewildered family, and indifferent others. Then I went to my barber, and the braids were gone, in favor of a conventional haircut.

Although the horsehair is gone, the memories of the trip linger on. From time to time, when I think of Maya Angelou or hear the name W.E.B. DuBois, or when a black teenager is shot walking through a Saint Louis neighborhood, echoes of that time rush in. At those moments, I feel some part of my forebears' saying, "Africa, where British anthropologists have determined human life itself originated—before populating the planet." While I am a Missouri native, I remember that a big part of my spiritual growth took place on "The Continent."

CHAPTER THIRTY-SIX

First Comes Love

INTERESTING THINGS SEEM TO HAPPEN when Sherry and I hang around with children's librarians. We often speculate that it takes a special person to be a children's librarian. Children's librarians are some of the most creative people I know; maybe it comes from reading all those picture books!

I met my wife, Sherry, at a storytelling festival in Atlanta, Georgia. Sherry said she was a children's librarian who told stories. She said that many of the stories in my repertoire mirrored similar ones in hers. I didn't know what she meant, but because of my heavy schedule, I did not have time to find out. A year later, at another festival in Woodruff, South Carolina, we sat down together and I found out she was right. We talked about our shared passion for storytelling over the last piece of coconut cake at our host's house. That day, I felt that

Sherry was someone I would want to keep in touch with when I went back to St. Louis and she returned to Atlanta. Two years later, we were together at an event on the Georgia Sea Islands. Walking along the deserted beach after sunset, I "popped the question." We married at yet another event in Lake Tahoe, California, seven months later.

CHAPTER THIRTY-SEVEN
Swan Song

ONE OF SHERRY'S BEST FRIENDS in Atlanta—and a co-worker in the library system there—is a woman named Mary Kay. Sherry introduced her as a dynamo in the library and an expert in children's literature.

The story I am about to relate is not, however, anything that might happen in a library, children's department or otherwise. I want to tell you about an experience that could only have happened out in the world of nature.

Further, this experience was not a stand-by-and-watch-it-happen sort of thing. This was definitely pro-active, hands-on, physical involvement. Remember this the next time you hear someone coo and fawn over how pretty, peaceful, and beautiful a swan is: *don't buy it!*

The place was metro Atlanta, Georgia, in a suburb near North Lake Mall. Mary Kay had recently had a baby and was on maternity leave from the Decatur, Georgia, Public Library System. Sherry and I went to Mary Kay's house to see the new addition to the family. We made a stop at the espresso shop for a morning soy café latté as we drove over to the house. We found the baby to be just as we expected—soooo cute! After a while, our hostess told us that there was a lake within a five-minute walk from her house. Excitedly, she said swans had been sighted there recently. Sherry opted to stay with the baby. Mary Kay took me to the lake to see the swans.

After a pleasant walk on a serpentine path through the neighborhood, we found ourselves at a small lake, probably one of those features a developer had added to the neighborhood to add charm. Standing there, we could see, perhaps 200 feet across the lake, a clump of trees and reeds in which two magnificent swans were nesting. If you are familiar with the behavior of nesting swans, you may know what was about to happen. I was new to the behavior of swans, and completely surprised by what happened next.

The larger of the two swans—later, I learned that it was the male—rose from the clump of trees and crossed the water, seemingly on a mission. He was gliding in a straight line ... toward ... us!

I was mesmerized by his reflection in the small waves on the lake. The symmetry of the perfect "V" his reflection made as he glided across the lake was hypnotic. His rapid approach caused me to divert my gaze from the beauty of his reflection and toward his approaching form. It took me a moment to form the right word for his expression. His eyes were set in a black mask that I decided looked decidedly ... malevolent!

The staccato drum beat of the theme from *Jaws* thumped in my head. Music from a horror movie seemed appropriate for the moment.

Mary Kay, who obviously felt the ominous overtone of the situation, quickly said, "Bobby, maybe we better go!" Still, there was a mutual hesitation because we both thought the swan would eventually circle and glide in another direction. Nope! That bad boy kept coming until he reached the shore where we were standing about fifteen feet from the water.

Landing at water's edge, he marched up the dirt beach, slapping one webbed foot after another as he marched on the shore … SPLAT! With timing that would have made Mr. Sousa proud, that swan's webbed feet found solid ground … SPLAT! SPLAT! SPLAT!

In my stupor I thought, *does it want us to feed it?* Suddenly, the large bird attacked Mary Kay, charging at her, squawking loudly, both wings expanded to their full and considerable length!

Mary Kay panicked. Understandably, she turned to run. But … she was wearing clogs with open heels. When the big bird tackled her, she tripped in her clogs and hit the ground, knees first. The swan then jumped on top of her, pecking her on the head, and stomping her shoulders with those large, webbed feet. All the while, he slapped her arms with both powerful wings.

Beneath the maniacal bird, Mary Kay curled into the fetal position on the ground, screaming!

I admit, in my high school and college years I had studied the martial arts. But Sensei never taught me how to do combat with an insane swan! Realizing that I had the soy café latté in my left hand, I threw the still-warm drink on the beast, yelling at it! For a few seconds, I could actually see rivulets of dark espresso and soy milk running through the white feathers. The phrase, "like water off a duck's back," went through my mind. The coffee, I found out later, soaked Mary Kay's shirt. Anyway, when I tossed the $4.70 drink on the creature, it stopped pummeling her and turned its hideous face and beady eyes on me! I thought to myself, *Uh oh, this is not good.*

Seemingly in slow motion, the swan stepped off her whimpering, defeated frame. It had found a more worthy contender.

My first automatic response was to take three giant steps in reverse! Like Field Marshall Montgomery facing the Nazi line, the swan studied his enemy. Me. His burning eyes were fixated on one purpose: how to subject me to the same thrashing it had just inflicted upon my friend.

Bruce Lee, Jet Li, Jackie Chan, and Sonny Shiba—I was now channeling all my Asian masters, steeling myself for the fight! All of a sudden I noticed to my right two fallen branches, each about four feet long, forming an X. As I stooped to grab the branches, the swan attacked! I stood up and thrust the branches in front of me, making a big X in the center of the swan's long neck. It slowed his charge—the audacity of desperation. Determined to defend his family—200 feet across the lake—he pushed forward, squawking, flapping his wings, and using that formidable beak—like the relentless shark in *Jaws*—snapping at me. It was a mortal tug-of-war. I pushed back with the X and he pushed forward. Perhaps it was a "push-of-war."

I pushed him back and he pushed forward into me. In the background, I could see Mary Kay get off the ground, staggering around, grabbing her shoes and holding her head.

Finally, the swan called a truce. He perceived a draw in the battle. Gracious in defeat, or at least in the draw, he nestled onto the ground, bending his legs underneath and folding his wings back against his side. That face and those beady eyes were still fixed on me, however. When we moved, he slowly rotated his head from side to side like a king cobra. When Mary Kay was within view of open space, she yelled, "Bobby! Run!"

Acting on pure instinct, I threw the two branches down in front of the great beast and ran full out back to our friend's house. We pushed our way into the house, exhausted and frantic. Mary Kay and I took turns interrupting Sherry and the cooing baby's previously calm, serene environment, as our versions of the story unwound in torrents.

As we attempted to explain what had happened, narrating and gesticulating over each other, we saw the horror—but also the silliness—of our adventure in the baby's and Sherry's wide eyes and open mouths. Sherry, on instinct, put the baby in my arms. Immediately, holding the infant calmed me. When Mary Kay went to the doctor later on, we found out her black and blue bruises indicated a larger problem—a slight concussion. After treatment, Mary Kay was released the same day with doctor's orders *for rest and indoor activity!*

Later, when I studied the behavior of swans with cygnets (young swans), I found the adult swans have been known to be very aggressive and will even try to pull dogs into the water and drown them if they venture too close to the nest. *Lovely*, I thought.

The following year, I went to perform at National Lewis University on the North Shore of Chicago. There just happened to be a lake on campus. I saw this sign:

Warning: Nesting Swans in the Area.
They tend to be very aggressive if approached!

Without hesitation, I strode very determinedly in the other direction!

CHAPTER THIRTY-EIGHT
Alaskan Adventures in Storytelling

ON MY VERY FIRST TRIP TO ALASKA—this one in late January—I was flying in to do a storytelling gig at the University of Alaska. When we landed, the pilot spoke over the intercom, "Welcome to Fairbanks! The current temperature is seventy below zero!"

I looked at Sherry and said, "Whoa!"

Then the pilot continued, saying the chill factor (what it felt like with the wind blowing) was 120 degrees below zero.

I said, "Double whoa!" I didn't think it could get that cold on this planet! Maybe Jupiter! After deplaning and locating our driver, we scurried to her car, making a united effort to get inside as quickly as possible. Trying to breathe in that frigid air was so wicked, it froze the inside of my sinus cavity. My lungs refused to allow that cold air into them. Startled, I gagged. Luckily, our driver and local-arrangements hostess brought us some male and female winter wear from her house. Her instruction was to wrap the wool scarves around our faces and breathe through the scarf. That worked. Following her advice, I was able to take in air that my lungs would accept.

Later, Sherry and I were delivered to our hotel and we checked into our room. Deciding that it was too early to stay put in the hotel, we agreed to do some exploring. We dressed up in parkas with hoods, mittens, wool scarves, and mukluks (Eskimo boots). Learning at the front desk that the Fred Meyer Superstore was two blocks down and three blocks over from the hotel on Airport Way Boulevard, we figured that walking there and back would be no problem. WRONG! We almost froze to death!

By the time we had walked those five blocks, our lungs were burning, our ears were brittle, and our feet and hands were numb. Even our eyelashes had frozen to our eyelids. Sherry's eyelashes looked bigger than normal, being "glued" to her lids. Modeling husbandly discretion, I refrained from commenting on Sherry's "new look," that she reminded me of a Betty Boop cartoon or a Big Eyes painting.

The tears in my eyes froze upon leaving my tear ducts. Once

inside the store, we were greeted by a blast of warm air, which was welcome indeed. A moment later, as we approached the fresh fruit, I looked at my wife again. Sherry's mascara was melting. The liquid mascara was running down her face, outlining her nose like a bizarre Halloween mask. We stayed in the store a long, long time. I felt like the Tin Man in Oz, in need of oil. I couldn't move! My body felt like it was on fire!

Every spot in the market felt warm. The breeze from the frozen meats section felt positively balmy. I was convinced the yogurt was spoiled, the dairy case being so warm. Then I remembered that I was comparing its temperature with the outdoor blast. I relaxed.

Finally, we summoned the courage to face the five-block walk back to the hotel. We managed to decline the temptation to buy grilled veggie burgers for use as ear muffs. We ate them instead and made our way back without losing any body parts to frostbite. We settled into the warmth of the hotel room with snacks, vino, and cable TV. The next day we tripled our layers of clothing, daring with only nine layers to brave the dash to our driver's curbside parking spot. The desk clerk saw us and exclaimed, "Did you guys stay up until three a.m.?? The Northern Lights were the best I've seen in several years!!

"Major downer," we said, "we went to bed at ten p.m.!"

Nature is endlessly fascinating. Listening to my body has allowed me to avoid major injury as I have moved through nearly every climatic region on the globe. Constant vigilance is the price of keeping one's ears, one's sanity, and centeredness. It is true in meteorology as it is in organizational politics: the air can get so cold it seems to burn the tissues of the body.

Today we have glaciers melting, droughts in the wetlands, raining in the deserts, tornados where none have been seen before, and monster hurricanes. In the parallel universe of American politics, seemingly reasonable people grapple with whether our human carbon footprint is scientific fact or a hoax perpetrated by some to deny jobs for Americans dependent on the fossil fuel industry.

Meanwhile, 2014 was been the warmest year on record in human history.

▲▲

To paraphrase an old saying, you can take the traveler out of Missouri, but you can't take Missouri out of the traveler.

Missouri-born and raised, I one day found myself called to perform in Alaska. Alaska is not Missouri!

Alaska's position on our Earth challenged my expectations on my first night there. In Missouri, I grew up knowing—not believing, but knowing—that darkness settles in sometime around 8:30 each summer night. That's when the lightning bugs come out to play keep-away from Mason jars. Yeah, nighttime was a big part of my summers as a Missouri-born kid.

Alaska is out to put Mr. Mason out of the bug jar business! On one of my many trips to Alaska, I was ushered into a hotel room with black curtains on the windows. Black curtains, must be they hired Dracula as interior designer.

Nope. I was about to experience a fact of life in Alaska, the strange phenomena of living in a place so near the North Pole that—in summer—the sun never truly sets. The evening sun sinks slowly toward the horizon, just as it does in Missouri. Then something bizarre happens … it hesitates, or appears to. The sun acts like a defiant toddler who refuses to go to bed. Yes, the sun sinks nearly to the horizon, but—like that toddler—refuses to go completely to "sleep." It hovers on the horizon until about four or five in the morning. Then rises again (!) as the planet rotates and the sun appears to make its southerly path from east to west.

Curious by nature, I rolled out of bed several times that first night to see if this midnight sun thing was for real. I had to experience it for myself. When I opened the drapes at 1:03 a.m., I was greeted by a beautiful evening sunset: a pale blue sky overhead, dappled pink and orange near the horizon. Just to see if Mother Nature was fooling with me, I popped up again at 2:12 a.m. There was the very same "sunset." Third time's a charm; I peeked again at 3:17 a.m. Still sunset!

The next night I decided to go for a 2 a.m. walk. People were pedaling bikes down the road, joggers nodded at me as they passed to the right on the trail. An elderly couple stopped to pick up their dalmation's scat. The parking lots of twenty-four-hour stores were full of pickup trucks, minivans, and sedans. Apparently, 2 a.m. is the shopping hour in Alaska.

Inside the first large store on my walk, I gawked at housewives stuffing shopping carts in which toddlers sat chirping happily. Outside, it looked to be two hours before sundown, but inside it was the shopping hour!

As 3 a.m. neared, I sat on a park bench sipping on an espresso and viewing the blue-pink sky, where cirrus clouds made their beautiful patterns in the distance. Maybe the locals thought it was the middle of the day, but I was soon overcome by exhaustion. The sleepy traveler, far from Missouri, made his way back to the hotel, closed the black curtains, and got some shuteye. By the way, espresso has no effect on my ability to fall asleep. Maybe that's why I kept adding more shots to my brew through the years until acid indigestion made me quit altogether. Oolong tea is my favorite brew now.

We were on a trip to perform for the Ketchikan, Alaska, Library System in 2004, when the children's librarian took Sherry and me to a cove on an island. She thought we might see a bald eagle in the wild. We arrived at a pristine Pacific inlet surrounded by several very tall pine trees. The view was stunning. We stood on the shore, heads tilted back, scanning the trees and the horizon. Our appetite whetted for observing our nation's symbolic bird, our heads rotated in hopes of seeing an eagle in its native habitat.

Then, out of nowhere, we felt a rush of air and a shadow crossed over our heads. A full-grown bald eagle swooped down between the giant pines and landed in the shallow waters of a barrier reef about fifty yards from where we stood. He began feasting on a salmon that was lying on the shore.

For a city boy and girl, observing our national symbol shredding flesh from a Pacific salmon—no small creature, itself—was like observing the Liberty Bell sound an alarm. Seconds later, the dramatic scene repeated itself as another full-grown bald eagle swooped in, flexed its powerful talons and began to challenge the first eagle for the prized salmon.

From our vantage point—plenty close to all of that raw animal force, let me assure you—we three humans were now mute with awe. Watching those two massive birds squawk and beat the air with their impressive wings, clawing and pecking at one another in mid-air, we were speechless. Four or five little black birds took advantage of the situation and sneaked on shore, eating on the salmon!

Shuddering before the display of raw might and primordial competition, we were torn between seeing the end of the confrontation … and withdrawing to the safety of civilization. Suddenly, we felt the winds dramatically change as twenty-five full-grown bald eagles dove between the tall pines and swept over our heads, casting their huge shadows on the surrounding landscape. Where two symbols of our national might had been engaged in what appeared a death-struggle, now twenty-seven of them circled before our eyes. The scene now became surreal, as these birds all landed and started a "council" of sorts, clicking and squawking in a mass of white heads and black feathers, encircling the two feuding eagles.

After a few moments, the scene changed dramatically. All of the eagles began to peck and feed on the same salmon. Obviously, some kind of hierarchy system or pecking order, if you will, was at play, though it was beyond the observation skills of humans to discern it. The children's librarian whispered to us, "I have lived here all these years, and I've never seen anything like this in my life!"

After their communion meal, the flock took back to the air, flying back to their respective branches in the surrounding pines. When all the eagles left, we three humans walked back to our car. The experience gave us stories to tell as we drove to see a totem pole that was being carved by Nathan Jackson for a business corporation in Japan. One of the talisman images in the totem ... the bald eagle!

CHAPTER THIRTY-NINE
The Elephant and the Dandelion

ALL OF MY TRIPS of this kind have been teachable moments and keys to the puzzle of why things happen to me in such patterns and with significance. I've had experiences that sometimes defied logic or rational explanation. Yet the patterns are so strong and the lessons seem always to be delivered as a "point of illumination," seeming to validate my decades of study in psychology, metaphysics, mythology, and naturalism. I see all of my experiences as clues to understanding my purpose at this point in my life, in the great historical and social progression, and in space.

On a different trip to Anchorage, Alaska, I appeared as scheduled at the Anchorage Zoo. Mo, the director of the Anchorage Public Library, accompanied me to the zoo for a photo shoot to promote literacy and increased youth attendance at the library. One of the main attractions at the zoo was a three-ton elephant, Maggie. Maggie had been rescued from poachers in Kenya. Maggie's mother had been killed by the poachers, leaving her orphaned as a young elephant. Now full-grown and a bit temperamental after her ordeal (according to her keeper), Maggie was chosen to accompany me in the photo for the library. Newspaper and TV reporters showed up for the event to capture her signature trick, playing an elephant-sized tambourine with her trunk and right front foot.

Mo and I found our place at the railing of Maggie's pen. Before us was an assembled audience of about 200 zoo visitors. We saw family groups mostly—plus three metro television crews, two radio crews, and two newspaper photographers. Eyes darted back and forth as everyone anticipated Maggie's musical show. Zoo officials instructed the library director and me to stand at the fence as the elephant keeper brought Maggie out to us.

As you can imagine, an elephant moves very deliberately. As we stood next to the low railing separating our position from the elephant's domain, I had time to wonder what it would feel like if the three-ton animal misstepped and squashed me like an ant! Dividing her three-ton weight by her four feet, I computed that she brought about 750 pounds of mass down on each heel, and that didn't include the force of momentum. My next thought was that I do not weigh 750 pounds … and I do not have an exoskeleton to protect my innards!

Zoo personnel drew me from my reverie, telling us that Maggie simply loved dandelions. A few minutes later, the magnificent pachyderm arrived, escorted by a keeper who gently prodded her with a nine-foot pole. When the elephant reached the railing, I lifted a microphone connected to the zoo's portable sound system to my lips and began to describe the stories I planned to tell. To add an educational element to the program, I asked the zookeeper to describe Maggie's daily routine. On cue, the librarian reached down and picked a dandelion out of the ground and handed it across the fence to Maggie. Maggie reached her trunk out over the fence and accepted the gentle yellow flower. Without crushing or eating it, Maggie smoothly and deftly handed the yellow flower to me!

A collective intake of air arose from the audience as I grasped the flower between my thumb and index finger and held it to my chest. A chorus of "Awwww" sounds was audible over the clicking of cameras as parents and paparazzi recorded the moment. I know Maggie wanted me to eat the dandelion, but seeing it was coated with pachyderm phlegm, I cuffed it and slipped it in my pocket. None the wiser, Maggie gave me two reassuring nods of her massive head, as if to cement the bond between us. Then she drew her trunk back over the railing, while four zookeepers ogled in amazement!

After my performance, I was told that Maggie was supposed to move on to her pen while I went to another area for my storytelling session. She had refused to leave the yard to go inside. Throughout my stories, Maggie stood on the fence listening to me several yards away drooping both of her huge ears over the fence, listening to the stories. While Maggie seemed to enjoy Anansi tales, a group of nearby trumpeter swans was not happy with the microphone sounds. The swans decided that it was their job to alert all of the other creatures of the field and forest to the presence of offending frequencies. But that's another story. The zookeeper later told me he could not persuade Maggie back inside her pen until my last story was over. Maggie, they said, had only condescended to turn tail and waddle back inside after the final audience applause.

Anchorage in July was hospitable for a storyteller from Saint Louis, Missouri, and for an elephant from Kenya. Sometime after I returned to my natural habitat along the Mississippi, I learned that, in the summer of 2006, Maggie was moved to a zoo in California. I suppose it was a more appropriate climate for a creature whose original home had been in Africa.

On our many excursions to the forty-ninth state to perform in the Summer Reading Club, we are constantly reminded of Alaska's natural beauty. Alaska never ever disappoints when it comes to adventure, awe, and dazzling scenery!

On one occasion, while in Alaska to perform for the Anchorage Library System, Sherry and I took a three-hour ocean cruise on the Gulf of Alaska, departing from Seward. Driving down from Anchorage, the ninety-mile run features glaciers and snow peaked mountains on the left. The ocean inlet (that many call Cook Inlet) and mountains are on the right. It was breathtaking view all the way to the town of Seward.

When we arrived at the docks, we boarded the cruise ship and the captain said, "Look at your booklets and see the animals that live in the Gulf. Hopefully, we will see a few." Well, the Captain was right! We saw whales, sea lions, puffins, and dolphins.

Then he pulled up about one hundred yards from a glacial wall. Someone said, "I thought I heard a crack in the glacier." The captain cut the engines and we waited, cameras poised. Suddenly the glacier "calved" and a thick slice of the huge wall of ice toppled into the ocean. The thousands of tons of falling ice created a wake that made our ship bob up and down like a one-ounce, red-and-white fishing float! As the foam bubbled across the surface of the water, people snapped photos, whooped, and cheered! It was later that I lamented the loss of the ice to the mother glacier. When we came back to the docks, every one of us was a satisfied customer. The ride back to Anchorage on the Seward Highway was, of course, as gorgeous as ever.

CHAPTER FORTY
Attack of the Killer Holsteins

FOR ME, ONE THE BENEFITS of being a touring storyteller includes exposure to various cultures, different ways of doing things, colorful customs and mind-expanding shifts of perspective on big and little facets of life. I'm also introduced to differing attitudes toward animals, even animals we consider very common. This story is about one of those mind-expanding—or at least mind-bending—moments.

Having been contracted to perform in the United Kingdom, I knew that our venue was what you might call an "out of the way locale." Flying into London-Gatwick Airport alone, since Sherry had to fly on a different flight due to work schedules, I knew that I was to travel by train to Cardiff, Wales. I was exhilarated when told that I had to catch three trains. I was eager to make this new adventure in the land called England.

One of the stations in which I would change trains was the enormous King's Cross Station that faces Euston Road on the north side of London. The imposing edifice stands nine stories tall and looks like a red brick castle. This is the station that inspired J.K. Rowling to make up Platform 9¾ in her famous books. The station actually has nine incoming rail lines. Silently amused, I roamed around the cavernous waiting area, pretending that I was waiting on the Hogwarts Express. However, I was not about to go running headlong into a solid wall, as in the books. Casually, I stepped over to a wall and leaned on it. I guess a nearby railway porter had seen this act of playfulness before on his platform. His bemused reaction, though masked in trademark British reserve, told me that I was not the first to mimic a scene from the book in this way. *I'm a silly Yank out for a bit of amusement,* I thought.

True Harry Potter fans know full well that the audio CDs with British actor Jim Dale narrating are largely responsible for the series becoming a modern fairytale classic with echoes of the hero's journey as based on Joseph Campbell's *The Power of Myth.* The subsequent movies were poor renditions of the original intent of the author, even though they were cinematic successes. Scenes and plot lines were altered in the movies for reasons known only to filmmakers, but the unabridged books and narrations on CDs are where the true power of Rowling's works shines. After contemplating all this, and lost in my own misgivings about being an African-American sporting the British surname Norfolk, I finally arrived—two connections later— at the final stop. I found a young worker of the Beyond the Border Storytelling Festival waiting to drive me to my lodgings.

Europeans and Asians place a car's steering wheel on the right side of the dash board and drive on the left side of the road, totally opposite of how we are wired to drive in America. Lots of curves and blind corners made the ride an eye opening experience!

When we arrived at the festival site, I found that it was a 500-year-old castle on the shore of the English Channel. Sherry met me there, having traveled on a different flight. Our assigned lodgings in the castle were called the Queen's Chamber. They consisted of a master bedroom, a dressing area, bath, and foyer. Access to it was up three flights of a spiral staircase with stone walls on each side. The medieval structure was complete with battlements on the roof, a great hall for dining, and a library where rare and ancient texts were housed. We had adventures with Dovie Thomason and Carmen Deedy while there, but that is for another book.

The first day we went out to perform at a Catholic school. After a hearty breakfast of Spaghetti-Os, milk and toast, our driver took us in her little Fiat by way of a serpentine country road. As we zipped along, suddenly we saw a guy walking down the same road, shepherding no less than thirty cows. Our driver came to a halt to let them pass. From the vantage point of our subcompact Fiat, a micro-car by American standards, all of the cattle seemed the size of elephants. As those cows ambled past on both sides of the car, they swung their udders as if to slam the side windows! Maybe they were just regular cows, they towered over that Fiat, each animal looking down at us sympathetically with huge, expressive brown eyes and joining in the cacophony of MOO! MOO! MOO!

Not all were empathetic. One knocked the right outside mirror off the car!

Several more MOOs resounded in our ears as the bovines— who clearly do not work by the job—plodded on by. Our driver, who said she had never experienced anything like this in her life, convulsed in a serious case of the giggles. Sherry, gawking through a partly-open window, caught a little cow slobber on the shoulder of her jacket.

The gentleman cow herder gave us a friendly smile and doffed his Irish cap when he passed. When we could finally see the landscape again, our driver jumped out to retrieve her severed mirror for repair later. Once again having the roadway to ourselves, we drove on into a lovely country day. On to our school!

Our blessing in life is that people compensate us to see places like this. Our work may be there, but the spirit always instills a bit of play into the adventure. When we are asked, "Where do you and Sherry go for vacation?" Our ready reply is, *home! I always envision Dorothy clicking those ruby red slippers three times!*

CHAPTER FORTY-ONE
Bell Rock

SEDONA, ARIZONA, has been known as the place where electromagnetic forces are emitted from the Earth and this vortex energy can be felt and utilized by individuals.

One my favorite places on the planet is this area. One day on a return trip from a gig in Phoenix, I drove to Sedona and went to Bell Rock, a well-known vortex site.

I parked the car on the road and walked the half mile to the bell-shaped tower in the desert. On impulse, I began to scale the wall of the butte. Never had I attempted a feat like this before. I slowly and carefully found a hand and foot hold on the sheer face of the rock, pulling myself up higher and higher. When I reached about one hundred feet, I turned my head to see the panorama of the Arizona desert from that height. Fantastic! At my altitude, hawks soared in search of small animals among the desert shrubs below, and I realized that I clung to a rock face far higher than comfort allowed.

When it was time to climb down, I could not find a foothold in the rock. My left foot could find a groove to descend, but my right foot was at a loss to find footing. As panic set in, I thought, *If I plummet a hundred feet to the desert floor, bones will probably break …*

and I will lie there bleeding from every orifice all night. Maybe tomorrow morning, a kindly hawk or eagle will alert the Forest Service of a body in the bushes.

I rested my forehead on the red rock wall, did slow deep breathing and went into a meditative state. I then put my right foot down and … it found a rut in the wall! I continued with the left and it found another rut. Like a blind man on a ladder, I slowly descended, as if I was an old hand at backward rock-climbing. Back on the level dirt, I gave thanks to the Earth Spirits and walked back to the car. I turned around to admire the climb—and descent—I had just made. I swear the indentations on Bell Rock seemed to form a smiley face that shone back at me as if to say, *Yes, Bobby Norfolk, you and the Earth are one.*

I gawked and thought, *Nooo … couldn't be.* I continued my walk and saw a small stack of stones designating a vortex. I stepped near the stones and suddenly I lost power in my legs. I fell to the ground on my back and broke out into loud mirthful laughter! I sat up suddenly and looked around, thinking that anyone who saw me would suppose I had lost my mind. Seeing no one in sight, I fell back laughing even harder.

Finally gathering my composure, I ambled back to my car, telling myself that this encounter would be remembered for a long time!

CHAPTER FORTY-TWO

Big Cats and Little Stars

I LOVE KITTY CATS but not when I have to transport a grown tomcat who does not know me and thinks he is my dinner, let alone mountain lions who may think I am their dinner.

While performing at Steve Sandfield's Sierra-Nevada Storytelling Festival, I was housed in a very nice cabin owned by a generous local couple. After driving through the infamous Donner Pass, a memorable passage for anyone sensitive to consuming meat in the first place, I checked in upon arrival with festival organizers. Then I proceeded to the first evening's activities, confident in my comfortable accommodations. The prospect of a quiet night of slumber seemed assured in my elegant cabin tucked away in its own secluded pine grove.

After dinner and a performance that first night, my hosts drove me to the cabin, chatting happily as I struggled to remain sociable after a long day of travel and an evening of storytelling. I was pooped! The sight and fragrance of pine trees stretching across a huge valley promised rest and rejuvenation. As we approached my cabin, I sighed deeply, anticipating some alone-time reclining on the second-floor deck, taking in the view of my pristine surroundings.

When I stepped out of the SUV, I looked up at the night sky and gasped! The constellations were out in full force. The luminous belt of our own Milky Way was more distinct than I could remember, perhaps since childhood excursions in Cuivre River State Park. My plan, after seeing the night sky, was to take a walk along the trail they had pointed out earlier, lie down on the ground and enjoy the light show of the heavens.

Concerned for my safety, my hosts warned me in parental tones that the area was inhabited by mountain lions that prowl the woods at night. Hmmm, I thought. After a nervous silence I asked, "Have there been reports of mountain lions in the immediate area?"

"Yep," they answered. "The local newspapers have reported attacks on medium-sized dogs and other domestic animals not far from here." And, "We have to put our two dogs in a fenced kennel so they won't be attacked." They then took their flashlights and billy clubs and walked to their house into the darkness.

Oh, this is good, I thought. I'm going to go into the woods at night, lie down on the ground and be potential mountain lion food. I'm going to spread out on the ground and lay some rosemary potatoes and parsley over my chest ... and wait!

Once I was alone, I assembled the protections at hand: a flashlight big enough to double as a club and a BIG STICK. I also tucked the kitchen butcher knife into my belt, pirate-fashion, for backup.

About a hundred yards outside the perimeter of the dusk-to-dawn yard lights, I nervously sat down on the ground and listened in the silence. Finally comfortable enough to look up, I marveled at the night sky, identifying constellations, locating the Big Dipper and the Little Dipper right away. Moving on to less-distinct constellations and clusters, I still kept my hearing totally attuned to a possible disturbance or rustle in the brush. Quiet ruled and the stars drew my attention heavenward. Eventually, recognizing that my heart rate was approaching a sleeping pace, I rose slowly and walked briskly back to the cabin, confident that my bravery crowned me—however privately—King of the Woods!

194

CHAPTER FORTY-THREE

The Popcorn Box or *Bobby in the Lobby*

ONE EVENING BETWEEN STORYTELLING GIGS, Sherry and I decided to take in a movie. The film we selected was playing at one of those huge multi-screen multiplex establishments that churn audiences every two hours, disgorging and engorging hordes of moviegoers, a true entertainment factory. The Northwest St. Louis locale was sure to bring us in contact with a crowd, but we were unprepared for the interesting event that occurred in the lobby.

Having stopped at the concession counter for popcorn and bottled water, we proceeded to the long, long hallway that would take us to Theatre Ten, our assigned auditorium. Approaching us from the other end of the hall was a group of "gang-bangers" walking in a "V" shape formation like geese in flight or soldiers on patrol.

People walking in our direction were "flown" against both walls as the phalanx separated and divided them. Regular people gave the V-formation cadre a wide berth. It seemed the sensible thing to do. It was clear that they intended to shove the theatre audience to the side walls of the corridor, so people responded as expected by withdrawing to the walls. It was the only option.

The leader of this intimidating group, riding point, was perhaps seventeen years old. He was attired distinctively in Hip Hop gear and carried himself with a swagger. This young man had attitude, and a lot of it. The posse behind him was made up of two "wings" of the V, each composed of five tough-guy subordinates, each equally confident that the hallway belonged to them.

As folks were slamming themselves against the walls like it was magnetized to their backs, I was convinced that we should walk straight down the hall toward our Theatre Ten.

Sherry did not think that was a good idea, "Do you not see that group of scary guys?" she exhorted.

"Yes, but we still need to get to our seats in Theatre Ten," I retorted.

She clung harder than ever to my arm, her vice-grip urging me to re-think my movement. Intuitively, I thought we should just proceed and ignore the V-formation that was plowing all others aside as it approached.

When I turned from Sherry's face to the face of the point guy, he and I made eye contact. The Intimidator stopped in his tracks. His eyes seemed to enlarge as he focused on me. His mouth fell open.

Pointing at me with a stiff arm, he shouted out, "Bobby Norfolk, the Storyteller!"

Turning to one of his underlings in the phalanx that had stopped abruptly and in unison, The Intimidator spoke to one of his cadre in the voice of a military order, "Let me borrow your popcorn box!" The next sentence out of his mouth was delivered to me, and in the voice of a supplicant: "Mr. Norfolk, can you sign this so I can have your autograph?"

You could have heard a popcorn kernel drop.

While Sherry and the whole population of stunned movie-goers watched in silence, I coolly withdrew a Sharpie from my pocket and autographed the popcorn box. As I handed the box back to The Intimidator, he said, "You came to my school when I was in the third grade!"

I said, "You were a little dude then weren't you?"

He grinned and replied sheepishly, "Yea, I was!"

Then one of his wingmen said, "I remember you from your TV show, *Gator Tales,* on Channel 4!"

After I had signed all of the obligatory popcorn boxes, The Intimidator and I bade each other *adios.* I said to the group, "You guys take care now." and Sherry and I continued toward our Theatre Ten. As I turned for a parting glance over my shoulder, The Intimidator and his posse re-formed and resumed their personas as they walked on out of the building.

That event on a day off stayed with me in my waking and sleeping moments for a long, long time. It became the defining moment, in which I saw what I do as missionary work, not just entertainment. It gave me a new perspective on my work, especially with the young. I came to realize that what I do—though some see it solely as entertainment—is important work. The folktales, poems, and stories I perform make a difference in forming values and beliefs. Since that day, I have listened attentively as teachers and students have expressed appreciations verbally and in letters, expressing what the V-shaped group said in this chance meeting.

Teachers have reported transformations in student behavior after my assemblies and all-day residencies. Principals even have reported improvement in standardized test scores. Occasionally, a school counselor will pull me aside to tell me about new attitudes toward achievement following my visits.

These reports of behavioral change and academic improvement at first seemed incredible. Sherry has experienced the same things in her residency work on a more extensive basis when she spends five days in a school. Now that they no longer seem rare, I have come to call them "small miracles." Now I see them as signs of powerful effects created by the power of storytelling.

How can that kind of interpersonal power be ignored? Why would anyone try to replace it or make it "obsolete" by technology? Even though I have never met fellow St. Louisans, Cedric the Entertainer or Nelly, someone asked me if they ever watched my TV show, *Gator Tales,* from 1988-1994? I can't say for sure, but if you know them, ask for me, please.

CHAPTER FORTY-FOUR

Niagara Falls

WHILE VISITING UPSTATE NEW YORK at a storytelling festival, I took a solo side trip to Niagara Falls. I drove my rental car for two hours to my destination. I purchased my ticket and got my boarding pass for the cruise on the observation boat, "Maid of the Mist." The crew issued plastic yellow rain gear, complete with hoods, when we boarded. Then the "Maid of the Mist" pulled out into the waters of Lake Erie. It was not long after our departure from the dock below the falls that we discovered why the vessel's name includes the word "mist." On one side of the boat, the United States falls tumble 110 feet with a deafening roar. On the other side, the wider Canadian falls make an even bigger splash. The captain navigated the boat near the base of the U.S. side first. Looking up at the wall of water cascading from the bluff above was awe-inspiring!

Scientists say that there is a beneficial effect on the human body from being there because air is charged with negative ions from the massive rush of water. Pure white foam formed on the churning water.

A constant mist rose up into the air, seemingly suspended there. It was all about us, saturating our rain gear and faces. Then the captain gave us a treat by pulling the boat over to the Canadian side, which is more impressive! When we got a safe distance from the north side, he now had us between the falls. As I gazed up and saw the water coming down, it looked like it was coming down in slow motion. I thought, *this is what Moses and the Israelites experienced when God parted the waters of the Red Sea.* That vivid image from the Book of Exodus, Moses and his followers stepping out between churning vertical walls of water, has long been a favorite Cecil B. DeMille/Charlton Heston movie moment for me. After the captain shut the engines down he exclaimed, "Ladies and gentlemen, this—is Niagara Falls!"

Like Moses and his people, we all stood between those walls of water, awesome in power and beauty. But unlike Moses, I had not lifted a rod and spoken to the Almighty. I was simply fortunate enough to live in an age when time and opportunity allowed me to witness a part of creation during my leisure hours. I was grateful for the time spent at the Falls. I drove the two-hour trip back to the bed and breakfast and supped in a quiet nearby café, completely lost in thought and appreciation of the natural wonder in which I had immersed myself—quite literally—that day.

CHAPTER FORTY-FIVE

Mt. Bromo, East Java, Indonesia

IN 2009, SHERRY AND I were invited to travel to Surabaya, Indonesia, to work in the International School there. The head librarian wanted to treat us to a special visit by going to an incredible area in East Java, Bromo Tengger Semeru National Park.

Mount Bromo is an active volcano. Pilgrimages to view the sunrise over the five thousand islands that make up the country of Indonesia are popular among natives and tourists, alike. Near the mouth of an active volcano, weather can be an issue.

When we arrived at the airport, we worked our way through customs. Our guide and driver, who also worked in our host school's security department, greeted us warmly. Almost as soon as we strapped ourselves into the school SUV, the roller coaster ride began! It was a several-hour drive to the base camp of Mount Bromo from the airport. The streets of Indonesia are extremely crowded with pedestrians of all ages, millions of scooters and motorbikes of all descriptions, even more bicycles, and everywhere we looked, rickshaws pulled by men on foot. I'm pretty sure we saw every bicycle ever imported to the country or manufactured there.

Our guide very deftly drove an amazingly consistent thirty miles per hour, absolutely unbelievable given the disorganized melee on every side of our vehicle. He exhibited such pure driving art, I was convinced the Petty Racing Team would give me a finder's fee to introduce him. I rode shotgun and Sherry was in the back. After twenty minutes, she could no longer watch out the window; it was too scary for Sherry. Every block of the city and every kilometer of the countryside presented a cultural or naturalist's surprise. Neither Sherry nor I wanted to miss this rare opportunity to see the local life, flora, and fauna of the island. In the back seat, Sherry kept peeking during the drive. In the front seat, I was having a ball! It was straight out of *National Geographic*—tiny streets teeming with people shopping at hawker stands and carts pulled by oxen!

Our driver weaved in and out of the crowded streets. Sherry and

I agreed that, if one of us had been at the wheel, we would never have made it to the volcano. More importantly, we would have significantly reduced the overcrowding on the city streets while simultaneously filling the hospitals, auto body shops, and slaughterhouses of the city in our wake. With the professional native at the wheel, we somehow avoided a thousand impending accidents and seemed to avoid even near misses.

"Near miss" is a relative term.

After an hour, we were out of the congested metropolis. After another three hours, we arrived at the base of the mountain. There, our serpentine ascent began. The driver and I had major fun swirling around hairpin turns that hugged the mountainside. Meanwhile, in the back seat, Sherry was impersonating a chameleon turning colors. While her stomach was in misery, her eyes were feasting on the view. She couldn't look away.

Upon arriving at the village, we enjoyed a pleasant vegetarian dinner and checked into a very tiny room with a space heater. After our entertainment-park-worthy ride through the tropical sun, we now found ourselves in a room in which undressing to shower for bed was not an option. The mountain air was cold at night. The space heater in our room was wholly inadequate. Fully dressed, we went to sleep in minutes, knowing we had to be up and out the door by 3:30 a.m. to drive up to the summit. My days of youth in the ice age apartments came rushing back full force as I slipped into a light sleep. Awakened by our guide with a tapping on the door, we arose, had snacks and coffee and got in the SUV. Arriving in the night ninety minutes before sunrise, we encountered people from China, Britain, Brazil, India, Canada, and Australia huddled in the predawn cold, awaiting the sunrise. Standing or sitting there, I would like to think that travelers from every continent were relieved by the presence of so many "pilgrims" from around the world. The final steep ascent was up a set of ancient stairs about 200 feet to the caldera of the volcano. With very slow deliberate steps, we walked to the top, stopping many times to regain focus because our lungs were craving oxygen in the aerobic attempt to take the summit.

After what seemed an eternity, we arrived at the top and looked into the deep- forbidding darkness of the volcano. Smoldering ash and soot slowly rose up from its interior. A guide said back in antiquity a sacrifice of children would be offered to the volcano spirits. Today they pitch in goats instead. Nature, like society, throws us curves at whiplash speed, even when a trusted guide is leading the way. The mysteries of Nature and this planet never seem to yield in their ability to astound me.

After sipping hot coffee, tea, and snapping a few photos with flash, the darkness in the east began to fade to pink. The crowds' anticipation was palpable as we jockeyed for a position for an unobstructed view. Overhead, the sky was crystal clear with stars, so we knew the sun would display its full wonder over the Pacific Ocean. We were not disappointed as the sun began to peek over the horizon. That orange orb slowly came into full view, spraying the east in radiant pink light. Shutterbugs all around us went crazy! As "oohs" and "ahhs" rose from the multitude, we realized that below us was a range of high mountains, with several volcanic peaks dominating our foreground. As their calderas and cones materialized in the colorful light, the "paparazzi" aimed their cameras and clicked away.

As daylight fully engulfed us, our guide and driver escorted us to the waiting vehicle. Then, our hearts full of wonder, we observed the mountainside beauties as he drove back down the mountain. Our objective for the morning was the desert floor, called "The Sea of Sand."

Small ponies that our guide had rented for us—with strict instructions to ignore the many vendors and hawkers rushing to sell this or rent that—would transport us through the seemingly empty desert. After mounting our ponies, our bodies became acutely aware of something very urgent. It was very hard to breathe! Engaging our spinning brains, we soon identified an overpowering sulfur stench. Reflexively, we resorted to short yoga breaths to suck whatever oxygen was in the air into our lungs. Once we adjusted our sight to the scene, it was like being on the moon.

Within the space of a morning, we had come from a mountain-top—a smoldering one—with crystalline air and distant vistas, to a desert sinkhole where breathing was a labor.

CHAPTER FORTY-SIX
Ball Lightning

EVEN IN MISSOURI, nature occasionally throws curve balls, opening our eyes to powers that invade our daily boredom, opening our minds frightfully, but with great beauty. But beauty can be fearsome, too. That was the case one day as my agent, Jan Dolan, and I were working in my St. Louis office. Jan called me to her desk across the room to look at something on the computer. I approached the desk and stood as she pointed out an email message on the screen. We discussed the business question that someone had written us about.

Behind the computer screen, a row of five nice-sized windows afforded a panoramic view of the pleasant yard and tree-lined side street. As she focused intently on the screen, my gaze was drawn to the window on impulse. Suddenly a huge ball of red-orange light, about the size of one of those Pilates exercise balls that people roll on during workouts, hung in mid-air. It hovered a moment above window level, then dropped and hovered for a brief moment right in front of us. Jan had not looked up from the computer, and I was too astonished to speak.

Ka-Blam! The ball of intense light exploded with a sonic boom and shattered into an invisible energy form, and it was gone! The concussion of the explosion knocked the large office clock from the wall over the computer onto the table, the sound echoing in my ears. Jan rocked back in her chair, screamed and yelled, "what was that noise?!"

How could I explain what I witnessed? Haltingly, I tried, only to see an expression of incredulity on her face. The office clock stood, frozen at 3:10 p.m., on her desk.

I went to the dictionary and looked up the phenomenon known as "ball lightning." *Webster's New World Dictionary* (2002) says ball lightning is "a rare form of lightning that is viewed as a short-lived, reddish glowing ball, up to about a foot in diameter. It appears to float in the air or move rapidly along the ground before disintegrating."

Energy is all around us, in more forms than we know. My bet is that energy within us interacts with energy "out there" more than we realize. On that day in Missouri, my respect for the varieties of energy grew by geometric proportions.

CHAPTER FORTY-SEVEN
Tinkerbelle

FOR A YEAR, Sherry and I lived on the seventh floor of an apartment complex on Euclid Avenue in the Central West End of St. Louis. One night, we decided to have East Indian curry take-out for dinner at home. Sitting down at the table, we proceeded to take the food from the bag and set the table. The way we were seated on either side of a corner of the table, there was a small space open at my left and her right. As Sherry arranged the plates and silverware, I opened the various food containers. With the Nan and Palak Paneer already set out, I opened the top of the aluminum tray containing the *basmati* rice. As I did so, a small sparkle appeared on the rim of the foil tray. What I saw was exactly like the brilliant sparkle one would see when a diamond catches the light, or when sunlight dances on a lake.

I was immediately transfixed by the light as it continued to balance on the rim of the container.

Suddenly, without any sound, it shot toward the corner of the room through the opening between Sherry and me. As it went in that direction, it left a sort of vapor trail—a thin, dark pencil lead-thin line about eight inches long—in its wake. It flew into the corner of the wall and disappeared. The vapor trail disappeared a half-second afterward.

As I sat, mouth agape, trying to process this phenomenon, Sherry asked, "Did you see that?"

Stunned even further, I asked her, "Did I see what?"

"Something just flew off the table into that corner!"

I asked her, "What exactly did you see?" She said she saw a sudden and swift movement in that direction, pointing toward the corner where I was looking.

She did not see that brilliant sparkle of light that I saw, but definitely the exit of "something." We dismissed a bug of any sort, as bugs don't disappear into the ether, leave airborne trails in their wake, nor glisten like diamond sparkle. That visitation did not return. Believe you me, I've been waiting for a Nature Fairy to appear again.

When the student is ready, the Master will appear ... in glimpses sometimes.

CHAPTER FORTY-EIGHT

Hagrid's Bug

In DECEMBER 2012, Sherry and I visited Universal Studios in Orlando, Florida. Our real mission, however, was to visit the Wizarding World of Harry Potter! Many people still have no idea that British actor Jim Dale recorded all seven novels by J.K. Rowling, unabridged. His dynamic and "magical" reading of those works has enthralled Sherry and me, starting with *The Sorcerer's Stone*. Jim Dale won a Spoken Word Grammy for *The Goblet of Fire*. In that audiobook, he created 125 voices.

We developed the habit of listening to excerpts of the CDs in the evenings because J.K Rowling, to us, became the master of modern mythology. The movies cannot come close to reading the books or listening to the audiobooks. Jim Dale is the reason why. He recites every word of the author, using distinctively different character voices for each of the Hogwarts people—plus his regular voice as narrator. When Warner Brothers secured the rights to produce the movies, they wrestled with J.K. Rowling about scene and dialog to fit the director's vision of the book as it should be filmed. Subsequently, in the movies, the director had too much license to manipulate scenes. When one reads the books or hears the unabridged audio, rather than seeing the movies, things are drastically different. A true Harry Potter aficionado is disconcerted that scenes were juggled so often, but that's Hollywood!

There is an urban myth about the meaning of author's initials "J.K." When I ask middle grade and high school students what the initials stand for, I get, "Just Kidding." I tell them that no parent would be that cruel to a child. It's actually, "Joanne Kathleen." The reason she used initials was that she and her publisher thought boys would not want to read *The Sorcerer's Stone* if they thought it was written by a "girl."

Once on the ground in Orlando, we suffered electric anticipation as we arrived at our hotel. The shuttle driver told all of us that the chance to build the Wizarding World of Harry Potter in Orlando was offered first to Disney. J.K. Rowling traveled to Florida to meet with Disney executives. Everything was going well with the details of the deal until it came to the Hogwarts castle. When Rowling started talking about the Hogwarts School of Witchcraft and Wizardry, and about the castle in which it is housed, the Disney execs allegedly said, "There is only one castle in Disney World" (the spindly white icon we see in all the ads).

Major deal breaker!

Rowling walked away from Disney, leaving Universal the opportunity to pounce. According to our shuttle driver, during the first year the Wizarding World opened, Disney's attendance dropped by thirty percent. Further, our shuttle driver said, the plan for Universal is to expand the Wizarding World to include an actual Hogwarts Express to carry guests around the park. Disney's revenge was to purchase rights to Marvel Comics and start a new park sensation on their grounds.

When we entered the Wizarding World, the original soundtrack music was everywhere. The Village of Hogsmead is just by the gate entrance. Its slanted rooftops are decked out in mock snow and ice. The familiar music from the movie puts you in the mood as you view characters from the books walking before you. Visual and auditory effects take the visitor directly into a three-dimensional near-reality.

A replica of the Hogwarts Express is on the right of the entrance gates, which are huge portals. The castle was every bit the image of the one visitors see in their imagination, while experiencing the books, the CDs, or movies. A fabulous ride takes you on a zip zap flight through the clutches of dragons, Dementors and the Slytherin Quidditch team.

There is so much more for a devotee to reminisce about, but what cannot be explained is an encounter Sherry and I had with a "very usual hovering being." As we were waiting in a long line to get on an amusement ride, something about the size of a very large insect came and hovered a foot or so from us. I stared at it in awe. It caught Sherry's attention too. It had one very green luminescent eye in the middle of its head and hummingbird type wings. As it hovered in the air staring at us, I slowly brought my hand up to point at it and it swooped quickly from side to side. I was willing to "visit" the critter, but not to be touched by it. Amazingly the people in front and behind us paid no attention, they just kept chatting with each other. I felt a deep sense of calm about the creature, and a curiosity. It did not have a drone type of hum; it emitted absolutely no sound. After we crept our way past Hagrid's Cabin toward the entrance to the roller coaster, it darted away and was not seen again. Sherry said, "I have lived in Florida for thirteen years and never saw anything like that before!" I was mystified too. What had we been visited by? It had no properties of a machine, but looked completely organic. Was it in fact a beetle-like drone sent out by the Disney execs to spy on the visitors? It seemed to be an unknown living being that radiated a green pulsating glow from one large eye. We sought someone who could explain what we had seen, but the park employees seemed to move in a stupor, going about their work of getting people on and off the ride. They did not see it either. We later contacted naturalist and storyteller Doug Elliott, describing our sighting in detail to him. Doug replied with picture after picture of what he thought it might be, but nothing matched. Some exotic insects came close, but no match. Doug contacted experts in entomology, the study of insects, which led us to the Entomology Task Force at the Schiele Museum. Here is what they said:

> "The entomology task force at the Schiele concurs
> with your estimation that it was a syrphid fly ...
> No other fits the description, although some of us
> went into some discussion of the term 'sweat bee' as
> another name. So, stand by your determination." In
> conclusion, Doug wrote to me saying "we cannot
> come to a final answer on the thing you saw so *enjoy
> the mystery* Bobby."

CHAPTER FORTY-NINE
The Hood

No, NOT THE ONE you may be thinking about. This story is about a car hood. One morning I was driving to a school performance in suburban Atlanta, about thirty miles from downtown. The Atlanta superhighway system is legend among motorists. Interstate 20, a major east-west artery of the Interstate Highway System, intersects with Interstate 75, an equally major north-south artery of the system, in downtown Atlanta. Interstate 85 runs northeast and southwest from Atlanta, creating another radial artery. Then there are Georgia 400, U.S. 41, U.S. 78, and "spaghetti junction." These and other roads contribute their traffic to what most drivers consider a real mess. A more or less circular highway, Interstate 285, known as the Perimeter, ties all of the mess together with everything but a big bow. In most areas, the interstates have sixteen lanes, eight going in each direction, if you count the very wide shoulders on these highways.

On a work morning, I was cruising at seventy-five MPH on I-85 North, headed to my school. My intuition gave a silent alert to look in my outside left mirror. A white Acura appeared behind me, closing fast. My intuition told me to concentrate on the Acura as it zoomed past me in the left lane next to the center wall. The car was doing at least ninety MPH and I briefly glimpsed four occupants as the car passed me. The sound of their engine roared in my left ear, then faded as the car sped up I-85 North. My intuition would not release my focus from the white Acura.

Suddenly the hood on the white Acura flew open! The driver's line of sight was now reduced to the small space between the open hood and the bottom of the windshield. I watched as the Acura's driver desperately tried to slow his vehicle down, which meant that the distance between our vehicles was rapidly diminishing. A red Toyota pickup appeared in my right mirror, pulling up along my right side. That meant my options to avoid the Acura had pretty much vanished.

At that moment, the hood of the Acura broke off the car! The forward velocity of the Acura and the force of wind at that speed caused both hood hinges to snap. Like a fifty-inch sheet metal Frisbee, the hood did a series of twirls in the air. Then, it's trajectory arched toward my windshield. Imagining the projectile crashing through my window, I gave one exhalation of breath. During that instant, the twirling hood inexplicably changed course. Even before I could react, the airborne hood struck my right fender with a THUMP. Then it skipped onto the right shoulder of the road.

By this time the traumatized Acura driver and his passengers were in the lane to my left, their car weaving erratically. As I passed them, I saw four terrified faces and then the engine compartment of their car. I was shaking as I pulled off at my exit, Jimmy Carter Parkway. Stopping at a gas station to survey the right fender, I saw what looked like the two small round indentations—three inches on each side, imprinted into the fender.

I was not at all concerned at the damage to my car, knowing I had just survived what could have been my decapitation and immediate death. Still, I wondered how the four people in the Acura felt. Having witnessed the whole thing and seen their alarmed faces as I drove past, I suspected they were in shock.

An ironic footnote: the Acura was white, the Toyota truck was red, and my car was blue. Yes, there was some patriotic symbolism going on, even as our lives weighed in the balance. Some would say I had been spared going to the morgue. I just said a silent word of thanks to The Master Within, took a deep breath, and headed to my school job.

A week later I had a vivid dream in red, white and blue. My dad, who had passed away six months earlier at age seventy-three, visited me. In the dream, he had a very young, handsome face and the wavy black hair of his youth. Waking from the dream, I remembered his claim that, with his pencil-thin mustache, he was so handsome during his high school years that the girls called him "Dark Gable," a play on Clark Gable, the famous movie star from the 1930s-50s. He wore a beautiful blue and red sweater, and the white collar of his shirt was showing. Dad swooped to my window and waved at me with a bright smile. His torso, however, was in a spiral or tornado form. I sat up in bed and called to him. He said, "It's not your time to come visit me!" After that statement, he swooped away. I woke up sweating profusely and found myself reaching for the window across the room. A powerful subconscious dream had found its way in full color into my waking life.

CHAPTER FIFTY
The Visual Beauty on the Windward Shore of Oahu

DURING THE FIRST of my library tours in Hawaii, I had to drive from Honolulu, on the leeward side of Oahu, to Kaneohe, the windward side. I was told that the windward sides of the Hawaiian Islands are much more lush and beautiful than the leeward sides, and that most of the rain forests were there. I would not know until I drove around the curve on H-3, en-route to Kaneohe. As I came around a wide curve, the Pacific Ocean suddenly appeared, opening up a huge panoramic view. I saw the colors of the ocean. Near shore, the water was a green turquoise. A bit further out, it turned deep blue. Deepening even further out toward the horizon, I saw inky indigo and then purple.

I sucked in air, my mouth flew open, my eyes got wide, and I tried frantically to find a pullover or shoulder of the road so I could take it all in. The state highway department knew this area was perfect for sightseeing, and a few hundred yards ahead was an overlook park. As I pulled in, I looked up to a view of cliff walls hundreds of feet tall. The black, jagged rock was clearly volcanic in origin. The rain forest was everywhere—360 degrees!

From the overlook, huge waves were splashing against the cliff walls, throwing plumes of foam and water into the air. It was a beautiful morning with not a cloud in sight. The sunlight radiated the aquamarine colors of the ocean to the pure delight of the small group of us standing there transfixed.

Being the explorer that I am, I had to go down the cliffs to the peninsula that jutted out into the ocean for about one hundred yards. Carefully, I found my footing between the rocks, avoiding the razor-sharp edges. People wearing flip-flops decided the sharp rocks were too treacherous and returned to the overlook. Outfitted properly with new hiking shoes, I would not be stopped!

After several moments pause to take in the view from various vantage points, I finally reached the part of the cliff onto which breakers splashed just ahead of me. The waves were three times my height and very powerful. The sound of the ocean beating against the rock was almost deafening. Yet it was also somehow soothing, calming, and awe-inspiring.

I was mesmerized by the waves and the power of the water as it recoiled from the shore. After a few moments, another wave would come and continue the rhythm with a massive crash-splash of foam, sound, and a huge spray of water.

I was so glad I had left the hotel extra early on my way to the library. The extra time provided me with the chance to sit in the presence of power and beauty that one does not see while landlocked in the Midwest. I finally forced myself to get up and slowly make my ascent back to my car, turning every few seconds to look over my shoulder. Gratefully, there were many more times on the highway to take in the view as I drove *slowly* to Kaneohe.

The bridge to Kaneohe takes you over a panoramic gorge surrounded by lush vegetation, tropical. Bright green, it contrasted with the aquamarine colors of the ocean—yet another visual extravaganza! I got a strange feeling of *déjà vu*—of having seen this before. Later, I was told the *King Kong* and *Godzilla* movies were filmed in this area.

There are, however, no primates or snakes in Hawaii. There were lots and lots of geckos, though. At dinner one evening, a gecko insisted on climbing up the wall of the open-air café and onto my table to share the food on my plate. I thumped the table, made my fingers look like a giant spider, anything to keep this guy out of my food.

Driving back to Honolulu, I retraced my trail and revisited all the overlooks—the rest of the day was mine. At one spot of shallow water, a giant sea turtle was being petted by surfers and sightseers. One of the native Hawaiians said the turtle was probably around 200 years old and had been seen by several generations of his people. This area is known as the Bonsai Pipeline, and twenty-foot waves were pushing their way toward the shore. I was told this is the area where the old police TV series *Hawaii Five-O* was filmed; *Book him, Danno!*

Some locals there practice an exceptionally slow pace of life in Hawaii, especially when compared to the hustle-bustle, get it done yesterday, rat-race, dog-eat-dog world back on the mainland.

I remember once, I was caught up in the infamous H-1 traffic headed to Kamehameha School, for a performance. When I arrived fifteen minutes before the performance, I walked swiftly through the school campus replete with lush South Pacific vegetation, gardens, and scenic breezeways. As I met the headmistress, she observed my panting. She knew I was itching to get the assembly going. Placing her hand on my forearm, the headmistress said, "Mr. Norfolk, it's okay. Let's go have a cup of hot tea and relax for a few minutes."

I followed her to the "Garden of Eden" that I had passed earlier, but had hardly seen. Now, I had time to take it all in and appreciate being in Paradise. She told her staff what time to have the kids down to the theatre, allowing time for me to compose myself. Then, she served Oolong tea and shortbread cookies as we discussed my technical requirements in the theatre. She eased the conversation to the joys of Hawaii and asked how I liked it. I submitted there were few other places on the planet more beautiful and relaxing. When I got to the theatre I was cool, calm, and collected. As the headmistress introduced me, she placed the traditional flowered lei around my neck. Then she hugged me and kissed me on each cheek. The Elders call this the "Aloha Spirit."

CHAPTER FIFTY-ONE

Bats in the Belfry

AT THE BIG SOUTH FORK STORYTELLING FESTIVAL in September 2012, Faye Wooden invited me to perform. Big South Fork is nestled in the Great Smokey Mountains National Park. We had two visitations of critters while there. Once was right at dinnertime in the main cabin. Faye, her husband, Lyn Ford, Kim Weitkamp, Sherry, and I were doing the "kitchen dance," preparing our evening meal. Suddenly Faye looked out onto the screened deck and shouted, "Bear! Bear! Bear!" We all jumped up full of adrenalin, looked out on the deck, and saw a yearling with her nose in the bag of garbage that had yet to make its way up to the dumpster. We thought we could wait until our evening dinner garbage was in the bag and make one trip up the quarter-mile path to the dumpster. Mr. Black Bear had motive, opportunity, and he was going for it. We all grabbed pots, pans, and ladles and started a cacophony by beating on them and yelling, "Get away!"

The bear looked at us like we had lost our minds. He stood up to his towering four-foot height, then dropped back down on all fours to continue his dinner. We got bold and escalated the situation. We opened the screen door and took our discordant beating and yelling to the deck. He bolted through the hole he had made in the screen, hopped onto a tree and scurried down from the second-floor deck to the ground. He would not leave. Five minutes later he was back up the tree, seeing if we had left. I got bold and started barking at him like a dog. He climbed back down but still would not leave.

I ran outside, barking like a dog, and chased him into the woods. Meanwhile, Sherry was yelling, "Bobby, come back here!" The bear didn't come back—until the next morning. We were at breakfast and all of a sudden he popped his head up into the front window, standing on the bench. We thought he looked too cute to chase away this time, so we let him be. When the rangers drove up in their vehicles, he ran off for good.

On ghost story night, we all arrived at the large circus-like tent and the crowd was spilling out of it onto the park grounds. I was on stage telling an Alaskan story of *Klooteekle*, a bloodthirsty creature who terrorized all whom it encountered. Right when I got to the point where the blood-sucking monster goes through a shape-shifting, a bat flew through the tent whizzing over my head three times. I ducked to avoid the dive bombing swoops with the audience gasping and thinking *This guy is good! Conjuring a vampire bat right on cue!* After it had left the tent, I did some improv for an audience which expressed its sheer delight.

Sherry, Kim, Lyn and Faye were all giggling at me and gawking at me like I was some sort of "Conjure Man."

CHAPTER FIFTY-TWO
Sharing the Fire

THE STORYTELLING CONFERENCE called Sharing the Fire is sponsored by the League for the Advancement of New England Storytelling (LANES). Once, a few weeks prior to that event, which was to be held on the MIT campus in Cambridge, Massachusetts, I had an epiphany. With only two weeks to go, I was preparing a keynote, still forming it in my mind. I realized that I was ready for the keynote *except for one thing.* My speech had no real ending.

That was a crisis.

Two weeks before the conference, I was scheduled to perform at a high school in Atlanta, Georgia. On that day in Atlanta, the keynote *finale* problem was running circles on the back burner of my brain. When I arrived at the high school, student aides led me to the arts complex where my performance would be held. A helpful stage technician walked me through the backstage area, before we did a sound and light check.

Returning to the dressing room for a quiet moment before the show, I noticed a green sheet of blank paper on a round table. A special track light in the room was even aimed at the table, illuminating the blank sheet of green paper from the back. Something on the reverse of the sheet caught my attention. Curious, I turned it over. There on the other side of the paper was the perfect closing to my keynote. It was a poem signed "Anonymous." Two weeks later, I used that poem to close out my keynote. The Cambridge audience reacted mightily, confirming that the poem was the perfect complement to the mission statement of LANES.

After the 30th anniversary of the National Storytelling Festival, I was asked by the National Storytelling Network to contribute some material for their forthcoming compact disc. Susan Klein, the editor of the audio-CD project, urged me to research the story's origin. We learned that the poet was James Patrick Kinney. By the time of our search, the story poem was in the public domain. We found that the original title was *The Cold Within,* and it was written in 1961.

THE COLD WITHIN

Six humans trapped by happenstance
In bleak and bitter cold.
Each one possessed a stick of wood
Or so the story's told.

Their dying fire in need of logs
The first man held his back
For of the faces round the fire
He noticed one was black.

The next man looking 'cross the way
Saw one not of his church
And couldn't bring himself to give
The fire his stick of birch.

The third one sat in tattered clothes.
He gave his coat a hitch.
Why should his log be put to use
To warm the idle rich?

The rich man just sat back and thought
Of the wealth he had in store
And how to keep what he had earned
From the lazy shiftless poor.

The black man's face bespoke revenge
As the fire passed from his sight.
For all he saw in his stick of wood
Was a chance to spite the white.

The last man of this forlorn group
Did naught except for gain.
Giving only to those who gave
Was how he played the game.

> *Their logs held tight in death's still hands*
> *Was proof of human sin.*
> *They didn't die from the cold without*
> *They died from the cold within.*

The first weekend of October 2014, I was a featured storyteller in Jonesborough, Tennessee, at the 30th anniversary of the National Storytelling Festival. On Sunday morning, I was one of five tellers at a Sacred Telling concert. I used some of the highlights of the Cambridge Keynote, which consisted of the power of story to transform lives, and finished with the poem. The tent of 2,000 listeners had been in a receptive mood to hear something uplifting. The applause afterward was longer than the poem itself. It was published on the CD, *Live and Thriving, At the 30th National Storytelling Festival.* The CD was produced by the National Storytelling Network.

STORY AND THE SUBCONSCIOUS MIND
An Afterword

IN THE BEGINNING, storytelling was just entertainment to me. I took the stage and did my thing. The audience took their seats and did their thing. Everyone went home with smiles on their faces. Life was cool. Then I began to research more deeply, digging beyond plot and characterization. What I discovered was that people are affected in significant ways by exposure to a story. Everything that we see, hear, taste, touch, and smell revolves around story. There is this primal thing going on in our brains that grasps onto narrative and connects us to this medium, as if we were plugged into a cosmic wall outlet.

The human brain is hard-wired to consume stories. Even before electronic devices were invented, families and communities would sit around the evening fire and tell stories. Something very primal was happening even then. Fire was the original light show; performers used it to quiet listener's brains from the distractions of the work world. As the fire drew imaginations into the flames, the story began. Time and space were suspended, nothing existed except the story. Whether the storyteller uses a hand-held microphone or a modern TV screen, the power draws the audience by the very soul from the cares of the day into the vortex of story.

One university study concluded that something called a *storytelling hypnosis* happens when people are deep in the vortex of a story. As the plot dances from scene to scene, the audience responds by leaning forward in their chairs: eyes widen, jaw muscles loosen and the jaw drops. Usually, the spell can only be broken by a major distraction, such as someone walking between the teller (or screen) and the listener. A loud noise behind the audience will have the same effect. That is why it is sacrilegious for anyone to arrive late to a performance … because they may break that spell.

In my travels, I have observed how storytelling changes children's lives. I have seen children diagnosed with ADD, ADHD, and with Asperger Syndrome, who seem to experience a metamorphosis when they encounter live storytelling. Teachers have approached me at conferences and workshops to tell me they have witnessed children with behavioral problems become immersed under the spell of a story well told, resulting in behavioral transformations—for the better.

We have a battle today going between the ancient art of live storytelling and technology. I am one of the proponents of live storytelling because I have seen the eyes of tens of thousands of faces light up during my performances. There is more going on than enjoyment, I can tell. Storytelling is an ancient art form that has withstood the test of time. More than that, it connects people on a level that electronic handheld devices do not. Community is more than a vague concept; it is a necessity for a balanced life. Nothing can replace community and nothing can supersede the influence of live storytelling on the human brain.

When Carl Jung developed the archetypes of human psychology, he studied whether the human soul resides in the subconscious or unconscious mind. He described the archetypes as the king, the queen, good versus evil, the witch, the dragon, and talismans. Talismans include the sword Excalibur of King Arthur, the ruby red slippers in *The Wizard of Oz*, and the ring in *The Hobbit*. When you examine even the most modern story—even one you strongly dislike—you will find Jung's archetypes—perhaps disguised under other names.

In his book *The Power of Myth* and the subsequent PBS special with Bill Moyers, Joseph Campbell elaborated upon the archetypes that Jung described. Campbell saw that mythology has the power to carry us *forward* as a civilization.

Ray Kurzweil, a futurist, believes that we have reached the apex of human evolution. He says that we have evolved as far as we can in human consciousness. He believes that we may need to have computer chips implanted in our brains to carry us into the next millennium as we approach "the singularity." This concept echoes the story of Mary Shelly's *Frankenstein* and scores of futuristic archetypal battle narratives, and the struggle between good and evil—such as that between humans and cyborgs in *Star Wars*. Narrative morphs in each generation, but is always strongest when practiced by a live audience confronting a present storyteller.

When I am researching folktales, fairytales, legends, myths, poetry and prose, there is an essence that I want to pull from each. It may not be apparent on the page, but I use my intuition to go beyond the printed page, gleaning elements from the story that will enhance its metaphysical power in the mind of the listener. My job as a live performer is to reach the listeners of three learning styles: visual, auditory, and kinesthetic. I want to help the visual learners visualize the story, the auditory learners experience the story through sound, and the kinesthetic learners through gesture and movement. Also as a creative device, I find and use meter, rhythm, and rhyme in the stories. Within the story process, I take the listener on a journey into recall, sequence, and imagery. This is not a mechanical process. When successful, there is a fusion of intuitive meaning that goes far beyond entertainment. When the audience is fully engaged, its members reflect deeply and approach a meditative state.

If you have enjoyed Bobby Norfolk's stories, please
take some time to visit:

www.bobbynorfolk.com
www.folktale.com
www.parkhurstbrothers.com
www.storynet.org